United Nations Unveiled
Goals of World Domination

Written by:

Alan E Shields

Copyright © 2023 Alan E Shields

Chapter 1
Introduction

<u>Motivation for the Book</u>

In this age of information and digital dominance, where every click, every view, and every digital footprint is recorded and analyzed, the power dynamics have shifted. We now find ourselves standing on the cusp of a new world order, one that has the potential to redefine not just international relations, but the very fabric of our societies. And at the heart of this intricate web lies the United Nations, an organization both revered and questioned.

Unprecedented Interconnectivity: Our era, often dubbed the 'Information Age', has revolutionized communication and collaboration. Satellite technologies, the internet, social media platforms, and now the nascent 5G and IoT (Internet of Things) technologies have compressed time and space. Today, an incident in a remote corner of the world can instantly become global news, echoing in boardrooms and living rooms alike. But, while this has fostered global camaraderie, it has also brought forth challenges. The ability to manipulate narratives, influence opinions, and even swing elections through digital means raises pressing questions about autonomy, freedom, and genuine democracy in this interconnected realm.

The UN: Savior or Overlord? The United Nations emerged from the smoldering ruins of a war-ravaged world. It was envisioned as a beacon – a guiding light that would prevent future global conflicts, champion human rights, and usher in an era of global harmony. Its Charter, with principles of sovereign equality and non-interference, reflected a dream shared by war-weary nations. But dreams, when left unchecked, can sometimes transmute into nightmares.

From its inception, the UN has been the center of numerous conspiracy theories. Whether it's secret meetings in dimly-lit chambers, alleged ties with global elites, or purported plans for a 'New World Order', the UN has never been free from the whisperings of the skeptical. And while some of these theories may sound like they've been plucked straight out of a dystopian novel, there are undeniable instances that fuel these suspicions.

For instance, the sheer influence of powerful nations within the UN's structure, especially within the Security Council, often draws criticism. The existence of veto power for a select few nations creates an environment where decisions can be, and have been, manipulated to serve vested interests. The question then arises: Is the UN truly an unbiased global mediator, or is it a puppet dancing to the tunes of powerful puppeteers?

A Tool's Dual Nature: Like the proverbial double-edged sword, tools can both heal and harm. The internet, for instance, democratizes information but can also propagate falsehoods at an alarming rate. Similarly, the UN, with its expansive reach and influence, can act as a global peacemaker or become a vehicle for covert control.

This book aims to delve deep into these concerns, unraveling the complexities and laying bare the underbelly of global governance. As we navigate through the chapters, we will critically examine the UN's actions, intentions, and the hidden machinations that some believe are steering it towards a goal of world domination. Whether you're a skeptic or a believer, the revelations in this book are bound to challenge your perceptions and ignite a spark of inquiry. After all, in an age of interconnectivity, it's not just the world that's interconnected, but the truths, half-truths, and deceptions as well.

Power, Expansion, and Concern

The shifting landscape of global power has always been a topic of intense scrutiny and speculation. Central to this narrative is the United Nations (UN), a body that has experienced a remarkable evolution in its influence, reach, and ambit of operation.

The Deepening Footprints of the UN: From its inception, the UN has been positioned as a bastion of global cooperation, an impartial mediator whose sole objective was to preserve peace and foster understanding among nations. However, as time has marched on, the tentacles of the UN have begun to sprawl into areas and domains which traditionally lay under the purview of sovereign nations. This infiltration has not always been overt; it often manifests subtly through international agreements, conventions, and resolutions.

This insidious seepage of influence raises a pertinent question: Where does one draw the line between global cooperation and an undue incursion into national affairs? Is the UN still the custodian of global peace or has it metamorphosed into a leviathan with aspirations that go beyond its original mandate?

Not Just What, But How: Every global directive proposed by the UN is wrapped in the garb of noble intent. Environmental conservation, gender equality, eradication of poverty - these are undeniably crucial objectives. However, for the discerning eye, the devil lies in the details. It's not just about what the UN aims to achieve, but how it goes about it.

Take, for instance, the adoption of environmental policies. While the urgency to address climate change is undeniable, the strategies and tactics employed often seem to disproportionately impact developing nations, thereby hindering their economic growth and aspirations. This selective imposition, some argue, is less about saving the planet and more about preserving the hegemony of powerful nations.

Hidden Agendas and Unintended Consequences: Behind the veneer of altruism, many see a complex web of political maneuvering and economic strategy. The policies and reforms pushed forth by the UN often come with strings attached – conditions that might benefit a few while leaving many in the lurch.

Moreover, the broad brushstrokes with which the UN paints its global directives often fail to take into account the diverse socio-cultural fabric of its member nations. A one-size-fits-all approach not only risks diluting the unique identity of nations but also sows the seeds of discontent and resistance.

The narrative of the UN's expansion and influence is neither linear nor simplistic. It's a mosaic of intent, action, and consequence. This book seeks to shed light on the darker corners of this narrative, hoping to unveil what lies beneath the polished surface of the UN's global initiatives. As we embark on this journey, readers are encouraged to question, probe, and form their own perspectives on the role and trajectory of the United Nations in the ever-evolving geopolitical landscape.

<u>Decoding the Narrative</u>

The idea of global governance has long been a point of contention among scholars, leaders, and the general populace alike. With the emergence of the United Nations (UN) post World War II, this concept was given a tangible form. While its initial premise was undoubtedly rooted in the noble pursuit of peace and international collaboration, the UN's trajectory over the decades has spurred a myriad of interpretations, and for some, apprehensions.

The "New World Order" in the Making: When one hears the term "New World Order", it often evokes imagery of shadowy elites controlling the world's levers of power. To its detractors, the UN's increasing influence and reach appear to be a manifestation of this concept. Its initiatives, which on the surface seem aimed at global harmony, are perceived by some as stepping stones to a monolithic global entity, stripping nations of their sovereignty and citizens of their freedoms.

Digital Governance - Efficiency or Entrapment? In recent times, the digital revolution has fundamentally transformed our lives. The UN's endeavor to be at the forefront of this revolution is evident in its strong advocacy for digital governance. While digital systems undoubtedly promise efficiency, transparency, and seamless integration, they also raise significant concerns. The data-driven world necessitates collection, storage, and analysis of vast amounts of personal data. In the hands of a powerful entity like the UN, this could translate into an unprecedented level of surveillance, overshadowing Orwellian prophecies.

Smart Cities - Utopia or Dystopia? The concept of smart cities, endorsed and promoted by the UN, paints a picture of a future where urban centers are hubs of technological advancements, ensuring sustainable living and unparalleled convenience. However, scratch beneath the surface, and one can identify potential pitfalls. The interconnectedness and integration of systems make for easy monitoring, potentially reducing citizens to mere data points, constantly observed and analyzed. In this matrix, the line between protection and intrusion becomes dangerously thin.

Centralized Digital Currencies - Unity or Uniformity? The global economic landscape is witnessing a paradigm shift with the rise of digital currencies. The UN's interest in this domain sparks concerns among skeptics. A centralized digital currency system could very well dismantle the unique economic identities of nations, leading to a singular global economic structure. While this promises stability and uniformity, it also potentially jeopardizes national economic strategies, rendering countries vulnerable to global economic fluctuations and decisions made by a select few.

The narrative surrounding the UN is intricate, riddled with nuances and divergent perspectives. As we delve deeper into its structures, policies, and intentions in this book, it becomes paramount for readers to remain discerning, evaluating the presented arguments critically. It is only through a meticulous examination of the unfolding plot can one hope to decode the true intentions of this global body and its role in the ever-evolving story of our world.

Why This Book Matters

In an era dominated by headlines, soundbites, and brief moments of digital attention, it becomes more challenging than ever to separate facts from fiction, truth from hyperbole. As institutions like the United Nations (UN) increasingly take center stage in global affairs, understanding their motives, methods, and end goals become not just an academic pursuit but a civic responsibility. That's where "United Nations Unveiled - Goals of World Domination" steps in, aiming to be a beacon in the midst of murky waters.

The Depths of Global Governance: While the term "global governance" might seem esoteric to some, it has profound implications for the everyday lives of billions. From the laws that countries enact to the international treaties they abide by, the tentacles of global governance touch us all. This book attempts to journey into its labyrinthine corridors, shedding light on the intricacies of the system and the actors who pull its strings. It's an odyssey into the heart of an institution that claims to represent the world, aiming to ascertain if it does so for the betterment of humanity or for its own concealed ambitions.

The Puppeteer Behind the Curtain: The UN, since its inception, has been projected as the world's moral compass, guiding nations through turbulent times towards a peaceful coexistence. However, as with any powerful institution, it isn't immune to scrutiny. Is it the selfless guardian it purports to be, or is there a puppeteer behind the curtain with grander designs than just global peace? As we wade through the content, this book will endeavor to lift that curtain, even if just a little, to glimpse the true visage of the entity behind it.

Conspiracies: Fact or Fiction? The world of conspiracies is both alluring and treacherous. While they often provide alternate explanations to established narratives, they also tread a fine line between skepticism and paranoia. This book delves into these shadowy realms, not with a predisposed bias but with a quest for truth. Are these theories merely the creations of overactive imaginations, or do they offer insights that mainstream narratives conveniently overlook? Our exploration aims to sift through the noise, seeking evidence, connections, and patterns that might lend credence to the claims.

The Altruist or The Strategist? A central theme that will run throughout this narrative is the dichotomy of the UN's nature. Is it the benevolent giant, tirelessly working for global welfare, or a strategic player, orchestrating events to serve its clandestine objectives? By examining its initiatives, actions, and outcomes, we hope to inch closer to an answer.

The path ahead is not just an exploration of an institution; it's an exploration of the very fabric of global dynamics, power plays, and the forces that shape our world. "United Nations Unveiled - Goals of World Domination" is not just a title; it's a mission, a commitment to unveiling truths, however unsettling they might be. As you turn each page, remember, this isn't just a book; it's an awakening.

Purpose and Goals

The allure of the United Nations (UN) as a symbol of global unity and peace is undeniable. Since its inception, the world has looked to this institution as the embodiment of international cooperation, a beacon shining through the darkest periods of human history. The tales of its humanitarian endeavors, peacekeeping missions, and global forums resonate with most, painting a picture of an entity diligently working to mend the fragmented fabric of the international community.

The Facade and Beyond: However, as is often the case with entities of great power and influence, there exists a dichotomy between the public facade and the mechanisms that operate behind closed doors. Just as a skilled magician distracts the audience with one hand while performing the actual trick with the other, could it be possible that the UN, with its myriad programs and initiatives, might be directing global attention towards certain issues while subtly orchestrating a different narrative behind the scenes?

Information Age - The Double-Edged Sword: Living in the Information Age means we are both blessed and cursed. Blessed, because never before has humanity had access to such a vast reservoir of knowledge. Cursed, because this very deluge of information can obscure truths, making it challenging to differentiate between well-intentioned propaganda and genuine actions. The role of "United Nations Unveiled - Goals of World Domination" in this vast landscape is akin to a compass, attempting to navigate through the storm of data, stories, and official statements to reach the heart of the UN's true intentions.

Demystifying Ambitions and Activities: While the UN's charter speaks of noble principles such as maintaining international peace, promoting social progress, and fostering better living standards, one must ponder whether these goals are pursued in their purest form or if they serve as a veneer for deeper, more strategic ambitions. By delving into historical records, analyzing patterns, and critically evaluating the outcomes of major initiatives, this book aims to unearth potential discrepancies between the UN's stated objectives and its actual activities on the global stage.

The journey upon which "United Nations Unveiled - Goals of World Domination" embarks is neither simple nor devoid of controversy. Challenging long-held beliefs and questioning the motives of an institution revered by many requires not just evidence, but also the courage to confront potentially unsettling revelations. But in the pursuit of truth, no stone can remain unturned, no matter how monumental. The aim is not to vilify but to understand, to look beyond the curtain and grasp the full scope of the narrative that shapes our world.

Unmask the Agenda

Beneath the Veil: The United Nations, in its illustrious history, has often been the spotlight's darling, proudly showcasing its myriad achievements. From halting wars to vaccinating children, its endeavors have been lauded by many as the pinnacle of international collaboration. Yet, every institution, regardless of its magnitude or reputation, has its shadows. For the UN, these are the spaces, obscured from public view, where decisions are made away from the world's prying eyes. It's in these very shadows that one might find strategies meticulously crafted to guide global narratives towards a particular end. "United Nations Unveiled - Goals of World Domination" embarks on a quest to illuminate these obscured corners, asking the question: Is there a puppeteer behind the curtain, manipulating the strings?

While the UN's peacekeeping missions resonate with tales of valor and its health campaigns echo with hope, it becomes imperative to explore the silences between these tales. What endeavors remain muted? Which strategies have been carefully veiled from the public's discerning gaze? Delving deep into these questions may reveal a facet of the UN that many might find unsettling – a facet characterized not by its achievements but by its covert machinations, each meticulously designed to subtly steer global events and narratives in a predetermined direction.

Dissecting Deception: In the intricate maze of global politics and diplomacy, not everything is as it seems. Beneath the shimmering surface of certain UN initiatives lie layers of complexity, riddled with ulterior motives that might not align with their outwardly noble intentions. Consider, for instance, an environmental conservation project. While on the surface it promotes sustainability and harmony with nature, could there be hidden commercial or geostrategic interests at play? Could certain nations or conglomerates stand to gain disproportionately, using the veil of environmentalism to further their ambitions?

"United Nations Unveiled - Goals of World Domination" doesn't shy away from these tough questions. Instead, it plunges headfirst into them, sifting through layers of information, policies, and actions to discern the truth. The aim is not merely to identify potential discrepancies but to dissect them, unraveling the intricate web of deception and laying it bare for all to see.

In the world of international diplomacy, the line between genuine intent and strategic deception is often blurred. By endeavoring to unmask the hidden agendas and dissect the deceptions, this book offers readers a unique lens through which to view the UN – one that goes beyond the official reports and media releases, delving into the very heart of its operations. Through this journey, readers are invited to challenge the accepted narratives, question the status quo, and form their own opinions about the true nature and intentions of this global behemoth.

Empower the Reader

Unearthing Information: In the digital age, where information is omnipresent, the challenge often lies not in its scarcity but in its overabundance. Navigating this deluge becomes even more taxing when biases, both overt and covert, influence the narratives. Mainstream media, whether intentionally or due to oversight, can sometimes overlook critical pieces of information, leaving gaps in the audience's understanding. These omissions, whether subtle or glaring, can shape perceptions, and consequently, the decisions made based on those perceptions.

"United Nations Unveiled - Goals of World Domination" doesn't just aim to be another voice in this cacophony. Instead, it seeks to be a compass, guiding readers to the often overlooked or intentionally omitted details surrounding the UN's operations. By unearthing these concealed gems, the book paints a fuller, more nuanced picture, enabling readers to see beyond the superficial and grasp the intricate complexities that lie beneath. Whether it's a covert operation, a policy decision made behind closed doors, or a piece of information buried in a report's appendix, the goal is to bring it to light, ensuring that readers have all the tools they need to form a well-informed opinion.

The Power of Knowledge: Knowledge, they say, is power. But in the context of global governance and geopolitics, it's more than just power — it's an armor, a shield that guards against manipulation. An informed populace is one that's resilient to undue influence, one that can discern between genuine intent and veiled agendas. By delving deep into the recesses of the UN's operations, strategies, and ambitions, this book arms its readers with this very knowledge.

When individuals understand the deeper workings of entities like the UN, they transform from passive observers to active participants in global conversations. No longer are they susceptible to being pawns, moved by the whims of larger players. Instead, they become chessmasters in their own right, understanding the board, recognizing the strategies, and making informed moves. Debates, discussions, and decisions, whether in the living room, the classroom, or the boardroom, become more substantive and informed.

"United Nations Unveiled - Goals of World Domination" aspires to be more than just a source of information. It's a catalyst, spurring its readers to think critically, question fearlessly, and engage proactively in global discussions. By unearthing concealed information and emphasizing the transformative power of knowledge, the book aims to empower readers, ensuring that they remain at the helm of their destiny, even in a rapidly shifting global landscape.

Stimulate Critical Thinking

Questioning the Quintessential: The United Nations, from its inception, has been lauded as the epitome of international cooperation, the beacon of hope in a world fraught with conflicts. Its very emblem — a world map cradled in olive branches — symbolizes peace and unity. Over time, this has cemented its position as not just a relevant, but a quintessential body, steering global affairs. However, any institution, no matter how revered, should not be beyond scrutiny.

In blindly accepting the UN's every move as an act for global betterment, there's a risk of overlooking possible discrepancies between their public image and their actions behind the scenes. Just as we scrutinize the actions of our local governments and leaders, so too should a body as influential as the UN be under the microscope. By spotlighting alternative perspectives, and pinpointing where the UN's actions might diverge from its declared objectives, "United Nations Unveiled - Goals of World Domination" attempts to jolt readers out of complacency. It urges them not to accept narratives purely because they are palatable or widely accepted but to approach them with a discerning, critical mindset. In doing so, it aims to foster an environment where readers don't just consume information but actively engage with it, challenging and refining their beliefs.

Beyond the Surface: Surface narratives, being easily digestible, often become the preferred version of events for many. They provide straightforward answers, require minimal cognitive effort, and conveniently align with established beliefs. But as any investigator or researcher will attest, truth often resides beneath the surface, shielded from casual observation.

This book champions the cause of in-depth analysis over cursory glances. By offering deep dives into the actions, policies, and decisions of the UN, it endeavors to peel back the layers of surface narratives, revealing the intricate web of motives and outcomes underneath. For instance, while a UN initiative might be presented with a noble veneer, could there be ulterior motives hidden beneath? Are there subtle power dynamics at play, which might not be immediately apparent? "United Nations Unveiled - Goals of World Domination" acts as a guide, ushering readers into these depths, encouraging them to probe, dissect, and critically evaluate the information they are presented with.

To truly understand the world and the forces that shape it, a passive acceptance of presented narratives is insufficient. Instead, active, critical engagement is required. "United Nations Unveiled - Goals of World Domination" aspires to be the catalyst for such engagement, challenging readers to question, to probe, and to think beyond the obvious. It is an invitation to a journey — one that delves into the depths, seeking truth beyond surface appearances.

Highlight Potential Threats to Sovereignty and Freedom

The Silent Erosion: National identities, with their unique tapestry of traditions, values, and beliefs, have been painstakingly woven over millennia. They are testament to human resilience, ingenuity, and the spirit of community. Similarly, individual freedoms, enshrined in countless constitutions and declarations across the world, are the cornerstone of democracies, fostering creativity, innovation, and personal agency.

Yet, as the world hurtles towards increasing globalization, there's a disconcerting undertow. Institutions like the United Nations, which advocate for global unity, may, inadvertently or intentionally, be promoting homogenization over unity, conformity over collaboration. The distinction is crucial. Unity respects diversity, cherishing it while working towards common goals. Homogenization, on the other hand, seeks to mold everyone and everything into a single, standardized template.

One might argue, "Isn't a unified global culture a good thing? Doesn't it break barriers and promote understanding?" On the surface, it might seem so. However, in potentially overriding indigenous cultures and values, this process risks erasing rich legacies and traditions. Moreover, when global bodies like the UN set universal standards or norms, there's a peril that these might not align with the values or beliefs of all nations. Over time, nations might find themselves subtly coerced into aligning with these standards, not because they truly believe in them, but out of diplomatic or economic compulsion. This silent erosion of national identity is a specter that looms large, demanding vigilance and critical evaluation.

Dystopia in Disguise: The digital age, with its promise of a connected, efficient future, is undeniably alluring. Concepts like smart cities, digital governance, and virtual realities tantalize with visions of a world where everything is at our fingertips, where global connectivity is but a click away.

However, this march towards digitization is a double-edged sword. With increasing reliance on technology comes the potential for surveillance and control on an unprecedented scale. Every online transaction, every digital communication, every virtual interaction can be logged, tracked, and analyzed.

The UN, with its push for global digital frameworks and governance, stands at the forefront of this march. But the question arises, to what end? While the stated objectives might center around efficiency and connectivity, there's an underlying potential for control and oversight that's alarming. The specter of George Orwell's "1984", with its omnipresent Big Brother, surveillance state, and controlled narratives, seems less a work of fiction and more a cautionary tale in the light of the UN's digital initiatives. When global bodies can potentially access and control digital infrastructures, the loss of individual and national privacy is a real concern. In such a scenario, the boundaries between utopia and dystopia blur, and the world might find itself sleepwalking into a reality where freedoms are not lost in a dramatic coup, but silently eroded bit by digital bit.

As the world stands at the cusp of a digital future, with global entities like the UN steering the course, it's imperative to be vigilant, to question, and to critically assess the trajectory we're on. "United Nations Unveiled - Goals of World Domination" aims to be a beacon in this endeavor, illuminating potential pitfalls and urging readers to chart a course that respects sovereignty and cherishes freedom.

In summary, "United Nations Unveiled - Goals of World Domination" isn't just an exposé; it's a clarion call to the world, urging citizens to be vigilant, to be informed, and to be ready to protect the cherished values of freedom and sovereignty. This journey will be revelatory, and perhaps unsettling, but it's a necessary exploration in these pivotal times.

In this introduction, the stage is set for a deep dive into the operations, mandates, and initiatives of the United Nations. The subsequent chapters will unravel the intricacies of the UN's strategies, exploring the potential risks they pose to the world's future. The journey might be unsettling at times, but it's crucial to traverse this path to safeguard the cherished ideals of freedom, autonomy, and individual rights.

Chapter 2
History and Formation of the UN

<u>Origins and Foundation</u>

The post-World War II era was a tumultuous period in global history. With the world reeling from the horrors of war, there was a palpable yearning for peace and unity. The birth of the United Nations was hailed as the dawn of a new age. But like the shadowy underbelly of a serene iceberg, there was more beneath the surface than met the eye.

Behind the Curtain of Goodwill

The Players: The creation of the United Nations wasn't a random act of spontaneity. It was a meticulously planned endeavor, orchestrated by key players whose intentions and ambitions, while publicized as altruistic, had multiple layers. The most prominent amongst these orchestrators were the Big Three - the United States, the Soviet Union, and the United Kingdom. These nations, bearing the economic and military might post-World War II, took charge of the reins, ensuring that the formation of this new global body adhered closely to their vision.

The dominion of the Big Three was not merely due to their active participation; it was a consequence of their sheer overpowering presence. They weren't just sitting at the table; they owned the table. Their influence was pervasive, reaching into the heart of every significant decision, every drafted resolution, and every policy proposition.

In this hierarchy of power, smaller nations found themselves sidelined. While they were present in debates and discussions, their actual influence was dwarfed by the behemoths. These smaller entities, despite having distinct cultures, histories, and aspirations, were often clubbed together, their individual voices drowned in the cacophony of larger geopolitics. This raises an unsettling question: Were these nations truly part of a collective effort for global peace and unity, or were they merely pawns in a grander scheme orchestrated by the giants?

The Birthplace: San Francisco, known for its iconic bridge and as a symbol of American freedom, was chosen as the birthplace of the United Nations. While on the surface this choice could be seen as a nod to a nation that played a pivotal role in ending the World War, it's essential to discern the implications of this decision. Hosting the signing of the UN Charter on American soil meant more than just a logistical convenience. It was a testament to where the real power lay. It indicated a home ground advantage, ensuring that the United States, one of the Big Three, held an influential edge from the inception of this global body.

In the Maze of Conferences

Dumbarton Oaks Conference: The gardens and estates of Dumbarton Oaks in Washington, D.C., bear witness to more than just nature's beauty. They saw the birth of the initial designs of the United Nations. On the surface, this conference was a meeting of minds, a collaborative endeavor to ensure a future free from the horrors of global conflict. But delve a little deeper, and you'll find a narrative not commonly discussed. The blueprints of the UN, drafted in this serene setting, bore the unmistakable imprint of the Big Three. These nations took it upon themselves to outline the skeletal structure of the UN, deciding its powers, functions, and very ethos. Critics argue that Dumbarton Oaks was less a collaborative effort and more a strategically orchestrated move by these dominant powers to discreetly lay the groundwork for a global entity they could control.

Yalta Conference: Amidst the picturesque backdrop of Crimea, the Yalta Conference was convened. Ostensibly, it was about charting out a post-war world, ensuring stability and reparations. But the attendees, namely Winston Churchill, Franklin D. Roosevelt, and Joseph Stalin, represented the Big Three, and their discussions went beyond mere post-war strategies. The conference was a tacit delineation of territories, a discreet marking of spheres of influence. It wasn't just about rebuilding a war-torn world; it was about ensuring that this new world order conformed to the aspirations of its most influential architects.

Security Council: The Powerhouse of Control?

The United Nations, in its structure, has various organs, each with its distinct roles. However, none has stirred as much debate and controversy as the Security Council. Often viewed as the epicenter of power within the UN, the Council's composition and authority reflect a hierarchy that doesn't necessarily align with the broader ideals of global democracy and representation.

Veto Power: Within the Security Council, the concept of veto power stands out as a glaring testament to this hierarchy. This unique privilege, extended only to the five permanent members — the United States, the Soviet Union (now Russia), the United Kingdom, France, and China — allows these nations to single-handedly halt any resolution, irrespective of its global support or necessity. This enormous authority grants these countries unparalleled influence in shaping global outcomes. While the intent behind this power may have been to prevent rash decisions or hasty actions, its implementation often portrays a different picture. Throughout the UN's history, the veto has been wielded not just to protect global interests, but often to further national agendas, block resolutions that challenge dominant narratives, or simply to maintain geopolitical hegemony. The very essence of the veto contradicts the concept of global unity, placing the whims of a few over the collective will of the many.

A Disguise of Democracy: At the heart of the UN's formation lies the promise of global democracy — a platform where each nation, regardless of its size or might, has a voice. The General Assembly was visualized as this democratic utopia, where every country has an equal say. However, this picturesque vision is soon clouded by a stark reality. Despite the cacophony of voices in the General Assembly, its resolutions remain non-binding, more symbolic than enforceable. In stark contrast, the Security Council, with its limited membership and dominant players, wields the power to enforce its decisions. This bifurcation of authority versus representation paints a troubling image. It hints at a possible facade, where the illusion of global democracy is maintained while real power is securely ensconced in the hands of a few.

Decoding the Foundational Principles

Peace and Security: The aftermath of the World Wars saw a world yearning for peace and stability. The UN's inception was painted as a beacon of this newfound hope. However, an ironical twist lay in the fact that the primary architects of this peace body were the very nations intricately involved in these wars. With these nations now leading the charge on global peace, one is compelled to question the sincerity of this endeavor. Was the UN's objective genuinely about ensuring peace? Or was it a crafty maneuver by these nations to dominate the narrative of global security, ensuring that future conflicts, if any, played out on terms favorable to them?

International Cooperation: Cooperation implies a collective effort, devoid of hierarchy, working towards a common goal. However, in the world of the UN, 'cooperation' often seems tinted with shades of control. From its inception, the power dynamics within the UN were skewed, with a handful of nations holding disproportionate influence. In this context, critics often argue that the UN's brand of 'cooperation' leans more towards 'coercion,' where smaller nations are nudged, or at times forced, to align with the agendas of the dominant few.

In summary, while the formation of the United Nations was undoubtedly a significant moment in history, heralded as a beacon of hope in tumultuous times, there exists a school of thought that suggests its foundation might have been laced with motives that were less altruistic and more strategic. As we delve deeper into the annals of history and the functioning of the UN, it becomes crucial to discern between the overt narratives and the covert intentions.

Major Milestones

The United Nations, throughout its existence, has been at the forefront of numerous global initiatives. But the surface narratives, for some, mask a series of moves in a chess game of power, influence, and control. Delving deeper into the major milestones offers a glimpse into this clandestine game:

Universal Declaration of Human Rights (1948)

The **Universal Declaration of Human Rights (UDHR)**, adopted in 1948, remains one of the most cited and revered documents in global governance. It was a response to the grotesque human rights abuses of World War II and aimed to establish a common standard for all peoples and nations. However, like many monumental texts, its interpretation and application have not been free from controversy.

Behind the Document: At its core, the UDHR was designed to champion the inalienable rights of every individual, irrespective of their race, religion, sex, or any other categorization. But therein lies the rub: its non-binding nature. This, critics argue, gives member states ample room to maneuver, allowing them to endorse the principles in theory while often disregarding them in practice. Such a dichotomy between intent and action raises an unsettling question: was the UDHR merely a tool for international optics, allowing nations to parade their commitment to human rights while, in many cases, doing little to uphold them?

Vagueness as a Tool: Another critique levied at the UDHR is its somewhat nebulous language. Certain terms within the declaration, like 'public order' or 'morality,' lack precise definitions. This ambiguity can be a double-edged sword. On the one hand, it allows for flexibility in application across diverse cultural and social contexts. On the other, it offers an avenue for potential misuse. Dominant powers, or even the UN itself, could potentially wield these vague terms as tools for exerting influence, bending interpretations to fit specific agendas or narratives.

Establishment of Peacekeeping Missions (1956 onwards)

The second half of the 20th century saw the UN stepping onto global hotspots with its iconic blue helmets, symbolizing its commitment to peacekeeping. These missions, initiated in 1956, were envisioned as neutral interventions to prevent conflicts and establish peace.

Purpose vs. Outcome: In principle, the concept of an international force stepping in to quell violence and ensure stability sounds commendable. Yet, the UN's peacekeeping track record is not unblemished. Reports of misconduct, ranging from financial corruption to, sadly, even instances of sexual abuse by peacekeeping personnel, have tarnished the noble intent of these missions. Furthermore, the selective nature of interventions — where some global conflicts warrant UN intervention while others go ignored — adds to skepticism. This selective approach, critics contend, hints at underlying geopolitical games, where the interests of dominant powers dictate the UN's course of action more than any altruistic commitment to peace.

Sovereignty at Stake: The very act of international troops setting foot on a nation's soil brings the concept of sovereignty under the microscope. While these missions are typically sanctioned by the host nation, the power dynamics at play cannot be ignored. Critics argue that, on occasion, peacekeeping missions have been less about maintaining peace and more about ensuring that the status quo, favorable to certain major powers, remains undisturbed. The overarching shadow of these powers, using the UN as a potential conduit for their ambitions, looms large over the legitimacy of some peacekeeping endeavors.

Formation of the World Bank and IMF (1944)

As the ashes of World War II settled, a new economic landscape began to take shape. Central to this reshaping were the **World Bank** and the **International Monetary Fund (IMF)**, both established in 1944. Envisioned as mechanisms to stabilize the global economic order, these institutions quickly emerged as power centers of their own.

Economic Saviors or Puppet Masters? The World Bank and IMF were presented as saviors, providing crucial financial support to countries in need, especially those recovering from the war's devastations. However, the cost of their assistance has often been steep. Numerous nations, especially in the developing world, have found themselves shackled by the stringent conditions these institutions attach to their loans. Structural adjustment policies, which ostensibly aim to streamline economies, have sometimes had the inadvertent effect of exacerbating inequalities and economic vulnerabilities. Instead of being the springboards to prosperity that they were touted to be, these policies, in certain cases, have plunged nations further into debt and economic strife.

Neo-colonial Accusations: The World Bank and IMF's influence doesn't end with economic prescriptions. Their dominance in determining the economic fate of countries has led many critics to draw parallels with colonial-era power dynamics. Such critics argue that, under the guise of economic guidance, these institutions perpetuate a system where developing nations remain economically subservient, reliant on the West. The notion of 'economic colonization' comes into play, where instead of direct political or territorial control, control is exerted through financial means, thereby stunting genuine autonomous development.

Millennium Development Goals (2000) & Sustainable Development Goals (2015)

The turn of the millennium saw the UN introducing a new set of objectives — the **Millennium Development Goals (MDGs)**, which in 2015 gave way to the more expansive **Sustainable Development Goals (SDGs)**. These initiatives were crafted with the noblest of intentions: to eradicate poverty, promote education, ensure gender equality, and more.

Benevolent Aims or Strings Attached? On paper, these goals are unarguably virtuous. Who wouldn't want a world free of hunger, where all have access to education and health? However, critics argue that the path to achieving these goals is paved with potential pitfalls. The strategies and methodologies prescribed by the UN and its associated bodies to reach these goals sometimes come across as prescriptive, almost interventionist. This, detractors suggest, is a way for powerful nations and global organizations to meddle in the internal affairs of sovereign countries, dictating terms under the banner of 'development'.

Development or Dictation? The very concept of a global organization setting developmental targets for nations around the world raises eyebrows. It begs the question: who gets to decide what 'development' looks like? The MDGs and SDGs, while universally applicable in theory, could be seen as embodying a Western-centric vision of progress and growth. This brings forth the critique of a potential one-size-fits-all approach, where diverse nations with varied cultural, social, and economic contexts are expected to march to the same drumbeat. Could this be a subtle strategy, critics wonder, for the global elite to shape the world in their image, dictating terms and ensuring their continued dominance?

Global Compact for Migration (2018)

In 2018, the UN introduced the **Global Compact for Migration**, aimed at addressing international migration in a comprehensive manner. It's a vision for safer, more orderly, and regular migration. However, as with most international agreements, the compact isn't free from controversy.

Beyond Borders: Migration has always been a sensitive issue, interwoven with matters of national identity, economy, and security. The ability to control one's borders and determine who can enter is often seen as a fundamental aspect of national sovereignty. Against this backdrop, the Global Compact, to some critics, represents an infringement on this right. The compact seeks to standardize the approach to migration, which some argue might not be suitable given the unique challenges and considerations of each country. Critics question whether the compact implies that decisions regarding migration, traditionally within the domain of individual countries, should now be influenced or even co-determined by international entities.

The Question of Sovereignty: Sovereignty, the bedrock principle of international relations, entails the full right and power of a governing body over itself, without any interference from outside sources or bodies. By promoting an international approach to migration, is the UN subtly laying the groundwork for a future where national borders become less significant? Is the concept of individual statehood, with its unique identity and autonomy, being undermined in favor of a more global, uniform system? Such questions have fueled debates about the compact's true intentions and potential implications.

The Paris Agreement (2016)

Climate Control or Power Play? The **Paris Agreement** stands as a testament to the world's commitment to combat climate change. The accord has been hailed as a groundbreaking effort to curb global warming and its deleterious effects. But not everyone views it through rose-tinted glasses. Some critics raise eyebrows at the underlying power dynamics of the agreement.

Climate change, while being a pressing global concern, has also become a tool in the global geopolitical game. The Paris Agreement, aiming to bring nations together in this fight, can also be seen as a sophisticated instrument of power play. Critics question the fairness of its provisions, particularly those related to financial and technological support. The argument goes that, while developed countries historically shoulder the bulk of responsibility for emissions, the agreement might place undue burdens on developing nations, both in terms of financial commitments and technological adaptations.

Economic Implications: The interplay between the environment and economics is intricate. Developed nations, with their industrial histories, are the primary contributors to global emissions. Yet, the economic implications of the Paris Agreement, some argue, may not adequately reflect this. Instead, critics fear that the accord provides an avenue for these economically dominant nations to further control and influence the economies of less developed countries. By dictating terms of climate action, are powerful nations also dictating economic futures?

In retrospect, while the UN's milestones are undeniably significant, they are also steeped in controversy and debate. For those who dare to look beyond the façade, these events offer a narrative of control, influence, and power dynamics that challenge the very ideals upon which the UN was supposedly founded.

As we traverse the annals of the UN's history, a pattern seemingly emerges: a series of initiatives, often veiled in the garb of global goodwill, that have the potential to centralize power and influence in the hands of a few. This chapter sets the stage, highlighting the initial steps in what many believe to be the UN's journey towards achieving a discreet, yet overarching control over the world's political, economic, and social landscapes. The chapters that follow will delve deeper, uncovering the layers that potentially reveal the UN's dystopian ambitions.

35

Chapter 3
Structure of the UN

<u>Key Bodies</u>

Delving into the labyrinthine structure of the United Nations, it's clear that the organization is more than just its public-facing initiatives and resolutions. Behind the convoluted web of committees and bodies, some see an intricate machine designed to concentrate power and influence in the hands of a few.

General Assembly (GA)

Often touted as the "world's town hall," the **General Assembly** is an arena where all 193 member states of the United Nations convene. This massive assembly reflects the very spirit of the UN, at least in theory. However, a deeper examination brings forward a few troubling points of contention.

The Illusion of Democracy: At its core, the GA operates on a seemingly egalitarian principle: one nation, one vote. This gives every nation, from tiny island states to sprawling superpowers, an equal say. But this facade of equality has its critics. The General Assembly's resolutions, which span a myriad of global issues, are not legally binding. This implies that while the GA might be a platform for nations to voice their concerns, major powers can, and frequently do, sidestep these resolutions without any real consequences. Such a dynamic, critics argue, makes the GA less of a powerful democratic entity and more of a stage for diplomatic rhetoric and grandstanding.

Influence vs. Power: The GA's annual general debates are a hotbed for stirring speeches, with world leaders articulating their national viewpoints on the global stage. However, the GA's lack of tangible enforcement capabilities casts a shadow on its influence. Nations are aware that real power often resides elsewhere, leading them to prioritize bilateral and regional dialogues over the GA's deliberations. Thus, while the GA might influence public opinion or shape narratives, it is not necessarily where decisions that change the course of global events are made.

Security Council (SC)

If the General Assembly is the stage of the UN, the **Security Council** is its backstage, where the real strings are pulled. Tasked with maintaining international peace and security, the SC's decisions carry weight. However, its structure and operations have become a source of significant contention.

The Power of the Few: Five countries – the United States, Russia, China, France, and the United Kingdom – collectively known as the P5, wield an extraordinary power within the SC: the veto. This means that any one of these nations can unilaterally block a resolution, irrespective of its global support. This system, while designed to prevent major conflicts between these powers, has often been weaponized for political gains. Critics argue that the SC, rather than being a true guardian of global peace, is frequently a battleground of the P5's geopolitical interests. The unchecked veto power, some suggest, is less about maintaining global equilibrium and more about perpetuating a skewed status quo that disproportionately favors these five nations.

Agendas and Alliances: The Security Council's track record reveals a complex web of alliances and allegiances. Decisions, rather than being purely based on objective assessments of global peace and security, often echo the strategic interests of its dominant members. Historical events, like interventions or the lack thereof in various global hotspots, provide ample evidence for critics to argue that SC decisions are often tinted by the lenses of political expediency and strategic gain. The veto system further entrenches these biases, allowing dominant players to shield allies and block adversaries, irrespective of broader global sentiments or ethical considerations.

International Court of Justice (ICJ)

Established in the post-war world as the principal judicial organ of the United Nations, the **International Court of Justice** emanates the lofty ideal of delivering justice at the global stage. Nestled in The Hague, the ICJ has been the scene of numerous historic judgments. Yet, its efficacy and true independence are topics of fervent debate among scholars and critics.

Justice or Just a Facade?: Over its tenure, the ICJ has been a theater for some of the world's most contentious disputes. Its rulings, often delivered after careful deliberation, are expected to shape international legal norms. But herein lies a paradox. There have been instances where its decisions, particularly those that don't align with the interests of powerful nations, have been sidelined. Such blatant disregard brings to the fore a pressing dilemma: Does the ICJ genuinely serve as an impartial beacon of justice, or is it reduced to a pawn, maneuvered by the strings of global power dynamics? If its judgments can be so easily sidestepped by those with clout, then its role as a genuine harbinger of justice becomes questionable.

Enforcement Paradox: The symbiotic relationship between the ICJ and the Security Council presents an intricate puzzle. For its decisions to have any tangible impact, the ICJ often requires the backing of the Security Council, especially the P5, to enforce its rulings. This setup spawns a peculiar paradox: The very nations that have the capacity to enforce judgments are sometimes the ones that flaunt or ignore them. This circle of power and defiance undermines the very essence of global justice, potentially turning the ICJ's rulings into mere recommendations rather than binding verdicts.

Secretariat

At the heart of the United Nations' sprawling operations lies the **Secretariat**. This organ, steered by the Secretary-General, oversees the implementation of the myriad mandates of the UN.

Shadowy Selections: The position of Secretary-General, often termed as the 'world's top diplomat', carries immense prestige. However, the process of selecting this global figurehead has its shadows. Instead of a transparent election, the selection is characterized by closed-door negotiations, primarily influenced by the P5. Such a setup ensures that the helm of the UN is handed to someone who resonates with the interests of these major powers. Critics argue that this clandestine selection process diminishes the chances of a truly independent or radical leader occupying the esteemed position, potentially suppressing voices that could challenge the status quo.

Organizational Control: Beyond the upper echelons of leadership, the vast bureaucratic machinery of the Secretariat drives the daily operations of the UN. Yet, the manner in which this machinery functions is a topic of scrutiny. Major donors and powerful states, through their financial contributions, wield considerable influence over the UN's budgetary allocations, appointments, and strategic directions. The dependence on these funds, combined with the outsized influence of certain nations, leads many to question the true impartiality of the Secretariat. Is it genuinely an independent organ dedicated to global betterment, or does it operate under the veiled influence of a few?

In analyzing the UN's structure, a discerning eye can trace the threads of influence that bind these bodies. For those who subscribe to the idea of a UN with ulterior motives, this structure offers a masterclass in the discreet concentration of power, masked by the veneer of global cooperation.

<u>Specialized Agencies and Their Roles</u>

While the United Nations' specialized agencies have been instituted to cater to particular global challenges, some skeptics see them as instruments for a more covert agenda: expanding the UN's influence and implementing policies favorable to a select few. Here's a closer look:

World Health Organization (WHO)

A beacon in the realm of global health, the **World Health Organization** has often been at the forefront of battles against epidemics, health crises, and the championing of primary healthcare for all. However, its structure, funding, and decision-making have often come under the scanner, raising questions about its true independence.

Influence over Independence: The functionality of any global organization is closely tied to its funding. The WHO, despite its global mandate, leans significantly on contributions from major nations and, intriguingly, private donors. This symbiotic relationship, while essential for the WHO's operations, also paves the way for potential external influence. Critics often question if this funding mechanism subtly guides the WHO's health directives. Are some of the organization's decisions, recommendations, and strategies purely the result of independent scientific deliberation, or are they occasionally tinted by the wishes of its significant donors? Such questions undermine the WHO's position as a neutral, science-driven entity.

Controversial Calls: The WHO's role during pandemics has often thrust it into the limelight, and not always favorably. Certain decisions, whether it's about declaring a pandemic or recommending interventions, have been perceived as delayed or shrouded in unnecessary mystery. While inefficiency could be a plausible explanation, a more sinister theory suggests these are not mere oversights. Critics argue that at times, the

WHO might be toeing a delicate political line, potentially sacrificing timely health interventions at the altar of global politics.

International Monetary Fund (IMF) and World Bank

The **IMF** and **World Bank**, with their vast financial reserves and economic expertise, position themselves as the guardians of global economic stability and growth. However, their interventions, especially in nations grappling with economic crises, often come with strings attached, giving rise to critical evaluations of their true intentions.

Economic Strings Attached: The assistance from the IMF and World Bank isn't just about funds; it's about shaping economies. Their loans come packaged with 'Structural Adjustment Programs' which dictate economic reforms. Ostensibly, these reforms are aimed at ensuring long-term economic health. But there's an underbelly to this. Some analysts perceive these mandates as tools of neocolonial control. By promoting an economic model that ostensibly benefits Western capitalist interests, they argue, these institutions are not merely aiding economies but shaping them in a particular mold, often at the expense of local needs and priorities.

Debt Diplomacy: The lifelines extended by the IMF and World Bank often result in nations being ensnared in a cycle of debt. As these debts accumulate, countries find themselves not just financially but also politically beholden to these institutions. This indebtedness, some claim, transforms into a form of diplomacy where external entities, under the guise of economic advice, exert considerable influence over domestic policies, economic priorities, and even political decisions. In this light, the role of these institutions begins to look less like benefactors and more like puppeteers, pulling the strings of national sovereignty.

United Nations Educational, Scientific and Cultural Organization (UNESCO)

The **United Nations Educational, Scientific and Cultural Organization** holds a mandate to promote global understanding through education, science, culture, and communication. Its noble endeavor to protect and promote global heritage is well-recognized. However, as with many global entities, the specter of bias and politicization does loom large in its undertakings.

Cultural Hegemony: UNESCO's role in education and culture is of paramount importance. By setting educational standards, championing literacy, and fostering intercultural understanding, it seeks to build a bridge between nations. However, this bridge, critics suggest, seems to be paved with a certain type of brick—a brick molded from often Western-centric values and narratives. The fear here is that UNESCO, perhaps inadvertently, contributes to a global culture that might marginalize or eclipse indigenous histories, traditions, and perspectives. This dominance of a particular narrative, they argue, doesn't just inform textbooks but shapes minds, subtly steering the global populace towards a homogenized worldview that might dilute cultural diversity.

Politicization of Heritage: The honor of being designated as a World Heritage Site brings with it prestige and often much-needed funds for preservation. However, this process isn't always just about historical or cultural merit. Some decisions regarding such designations or, conversely, the decision to withhold such a status, seem to reek of political influence. Critics argue that UNESCO's decisions, at times, seem to be tethered to geopolitical dynamics rather than purely cultural or historical significance. This politicization, if true, undermines the very essence of global heritage, converting it from a testament of human achievement to a pawn in global diplomacy.

Food and Agriculture Organization (FAO)

As the global guardian of food security and agricultural development, the **Food and Agriculture Organization** has a crucial role in ensuring that the world's populace has access to adequate, safe, and nutritious food. But the pathways it chooses to achieve this noble goal have often been the subject of scrutiny.

Industrial Over Indigenous: Modern farming techniques, with their promise of higher yields, have revolutionized agriculture. The FAO's push for such methods is seen by many as a pragmatic approach to combat global hunger. However, the other side of this coin, some argue, is the gradual sidelining of traditional farming practices that have sustained communities for generations. These indigenous methods, often more in tune with local ecosystems, are replaced by an industrialized farming template which critics argue disproportionately benefits multinational agribusinesses. This shift not only jeopardizes the livelihoods of local farmers but might also lead to a loss of biodiversity, as local crop varieties make way for mass-produced alternatives.

Genetic Manipulation Concerns: The realm of genetically modified organisms is a contentious one. The FAO's stance on GMOs, especially its collaborations with certain biotech giants, is a significant bone of contention. While GMOs promise increased yields and resistance to pests, the consolidation of seed production under a few corporate entities raises alarm bells. Critics argue that by endorsing a specific agricultural model, the FAO may inadvertently be strengthening corporate strangleholds on the food supply chain. This not only poses economic concerns but touches on the very sovereignty of nations. If a country's food supply is heavily dependent on patented seeds controlled by a few companies, where does it leave its food security and autonomy?

As these specialized agencies of the UN chart their courses, it becomes essential for observers to discern between genuine global welfare initiatives and potential overreaches. For the skeptic, these agencies represent yet another layer in the intricate tapestry of the UN's purported ambitions of global dominance.

The intricate design of the UN, with its multitude of bodies and specialized agencies, presents a façade of diversity and specialization. However, beneath this façade, as this chapter seeks to highlight, lie mechanisms that potentially allow for control, influence, and the furthering of interests by a select few. As we delve deeper into the UN's specific initiatives in the subsequent chapters, these patterns of control and influence become even more pronounced.

Chapter 4
Evidence of UN's Global Influence

<u>Past Instances of Influence and Control</u>

While the United Nations has always professed its adherence to principles of neutrality, peace, and global collaboration, its history presents moments that, for skeptics, suggest a more manipulative role. Whether it's direct intervention or more covert methods, the UN has been at the center of numerous controversies that hint at an agenda beyond its stated missions.

Intervention in Domestic Conflicts

The Korean Imbroglio: In the wake of World War II, as the Cold War began to shape international relations, the Korean Peninsula emerged as a hotspot. The Korean War (1950-1953) saw the North, backed by communist allies, pitted against the South, supported by the Western bloc. The UN's involvement, championed by the Security Council, is often painted as a response to North Korean aggression. However, the dynamics weren't that straightforward. The fact that a significant Security Council decision could be made due to the absence of the Soviet Union (due to a boycott) exposes a flaw in the very mechanism that is supposed to safeguard global peace. The UN forces, despite the diverse flag-bearing, were overwhelmingly American in composition and command. This has led to interpretations that the UN, in this instance, acted as a cloak, shielding the strategic ambitions of a major power rather than serving as an unbiased mediator.

Beyond Korea: The Congo Crisis of the early 1960s serves as another instance where the lines between international intervention and interference blur. A nation grappling with the vestiges of colonialism witnessed a complex interplay of secessionist movements, assassinations, and Cold War politics. The UN's involvement, while initially humanitarian, evolved into a more active role, including military operations against secessionist forces. This level of engagement in a nation's internal affairs opens the door to the argument that the UN, under the guise of peacekeeping, sometimes encroaches upon national sovereignties.

Economic Sanctions

The Iraqi Quagmire: The 1990s saw Iraq under the spotlight, following its invasion of Kuwait. The Gulf War, and Iraq's subsequent defeat, led to a slew of UN-imposed sanctions. While the stated objective was to curtail Iraq's weapons programs, the ramifications went far beyond. The civilian suffering, as a result of these economic constraints, was profound. Malnutrition, lack of medical supplies, and deteriorating infrastructure became emblematic of a nation in distress. Critics of the UN's approach argue that the sanctions became a weapon of the West, particularly the US, to keep an adversarial regime in check, with the UN merely acting as a legitimizing platform.

Sanctions Elsewhere: The UN's track record with sanctions isn't limited to Iraq. Be it North Korea, grappling with food shortages, or Iran, with its constrained economy, the tale is eerily similar. The sanctions, often backed by major powers in the Security Council, tend to have a cascading impact on civilian lives. The selective imposition of these sanctions, often targeting nations that defy Western interests, raises the question: Are these genuinely tools for global justice or instruments of geopolitics, wielded by the powerful?

Peacekeeping Missions Gone Awry

Rwandan Catastrophe: 1994 remains an indelibly dark year in modern history, where humanity witnessed one of the most brutal genocides in Rwanda. Close to a million Tutsis fell victim to ethnic violence, and what remains a chilling testament to international apathy is that this occurred under the very nose of the UN. Despite clear indications of escalating violence, the United Nations Assistance Mission for Rwanda (UNAMIR) was neither strengthened nor given a mandate robust enough to intervene. The painful irony is that the 'peacekeepers' were more spectators than guardians. The international community's and by extension the UN's hesitancy to act decisively has made Rwanda a haunting example of global inaction in the face of clear and imminent disaster.

Balkan Brutality: The Balkans in the 1990s was a melting pot of ethnic tensions and historical grudges. As Yugoslavia disintegrated, Bosnia emerged as a battleground of brutal proportions. The UN's creation of "safe areas" was seen as a beacon of hope amidst the storm, but these very zones, especially Srebrenica, would go on to become graveyards. The harrowing massacre of over 8,000 Bosniak men in Srebrenica, a declared UN-protected area, unveiled the gaping holes in the UN's peacekeeping machinery. Was this a mere oversight, a case of being under-resourced, or did it hint at a deeper malaise of a UN that could be rendered ineffective when superpowers played their geopolitical games?

Overthrow of Leaders

Libyan Crisis: The Libyan narrative of 2011 is a study in how international interventions, under the banner of humanitarian causes, can go awry. The UN Security Council, backed by Western powers, advocated for a mission to protect Libyan civilians amidst a rebellion against Muammar Gaddafi's regime. Yet, in what seemed like a rapid turn of events, the mission's objective seemed to shift from protection to regime change. The death of Gaddafi, rather than ushering in an era of peace, led to a power vacuum. Today's Libya, rife with extremism, factional wars, and a hotbed for human trafficking, stands as a testament to the unforeseen consequences of what critics label as the UN's manipulated mandate. Was Libya a genuine effort gone wrong or a veiled attempt at regime change with the UN as its facade?

Regime Changes and the UN: Direct coups or overthrows backed by the UN are scarce. However, the notion persists that the institution's various mandates, especially those around peacekeeping and intervention, provide ample gray areas that powerful states can exploit. By bending the rules or interpreting mandates to their advantage, these states, critics argue, leverage the UN's global legitimacy to further their geostrategic ambitions, often at the cost of smaller, less influential nations.

The evidence, skeptics assert, suggests a pattern where the UN, intentionally or otherwise, becomes an instrument in the hands of influential members. Far from being a neutral arbiter of global peace, it appears, at times, to be a player in the very geopolitical games it seeks to mediate.

Comparison of UN's Actions Across Different Regions

The seeming inconsistencies in the UN's approach across different continents have fueled the perception that its interventions, or lack thereof, are influenced by hidden agendas or major powers, rather than being based purely on humanitarian or peacekeeping considerations.

Middle East: A Complex Theatre

The Israel-Palestine Conundrum: The Israel-Palestine conflict has been a contentious issue that has simmered, flared, and persisted over decades. The UN's role in this quagmire is deeply controversial. Many note that the organization has passed a disproportionate number of resolutions critical of Israel. While there is little doubt about the contentious nature of Israel's actions, especially in occupied territories, what raises eyebrows is the selective intensity of focus. Atrocities of similar or even graver magnitude in other parts of the world often don't seem to elicit the same degree of censure. This discrepancy feeds into the narrative that the UN, rather than being a neutral arbitrator, is a tool in the larger geopolitical game, with Israel often in the crosshairs. Such perspectives foster an image of the UN as an institution that can be wielded against nations that are out of favor with powerful members.

Syrian Civil War: The Syrian conflict is a heartrending tale of human suffering, a proxy war, and international apathy. As the nation bled and millions sought refuge worldwide, the UN largely remained on the sidelines. Numerous attempts to broker peace, initiate ceasefires, or even merely condemn actions were stonewalled, mainly by vetoes from permanent members of the Security Council. Here, the UN's structure, which gives disproportionate power to its permanent members, was exposed. The Syrian debacle underscores that the UN, regardless of its global mandate, can be rendered impotent if major powers, for their strategic reasons, wish to stall action.

Africa: A Mosaic of Intervention and Neglect

Rwandan Genocide: When one speaks of UN's failures, the Rwandan Genocide often stands out as a stark illustration. 1994 wasn't just a failure of humanity at large but exposed the cracks in the UN's commitment to its foundational goals. Despite distress signals and clear indications of an impending catastrophe, the UN's response was marked by hesitation and bureaucracy. Critics argue that the sluggishness wasn't merely a procedural lapse. They contend that major powers, lacking any significant strategic stakes in Rwanda, were indifferent, thus influencing the UN's response or lack thereof.

Resource Diplomacy: Africa, a continent rich in minerals and natural resources, has been the arena of numerous interventions. From diamonds in Sierra Leone to coltan in the Congo, the continent's vast wealth has often caught global attention. Many interventions, often wearing the mask of peacekeeping, humanitarian aid, or developmental projects, have been initiated under the UN's banner. Yet, skeptics note a pattern. These interventions, rather than solely focusing on the well-being of the local populace, seem to ensure that Africa's resources remain within the grasp of Western corporations. The very structure of some UN-backed initiatives, critics argue, facilitates a neo-colonial economic model, where African nations provide the raw materials, but the profits and benefits flow outwards, perpetuating a cycle of dependency and exploitation.

Conclusion:

Across these diverse regions, a picture emerges of the UN's actions (or inactions) being less about universal principles and more influenced by the geopolitical interests of its most powerful members. This examination, while focusing on past instances, compels us to question if the UN in its present form is indeed a beacon of hope and justice or if it's a stage where global power games play out, often at the expense of the vulnerable.

Asia: Selective Engagements

Rohingya Crisis: The mass exodus and ethnic cleansing of the Rohingya community in Myanmar brought to the fore not just the brutality of such actions but also the apparent inertia of the UN. While the situation garnered global headlines, the UN's response seemed to lack the urgency and potency that such a dire situation warranted. Critics argue that the organization's reaction was a mere shadow of what it could and should have been. They contend that had this crisis occurred in a region that was geographically or geopolitically closer to the vested interests of major powers, the response might have been far more immediate and assertive. This differential reaction underscores the belief among some quarters that the UN's actions—or lack thereof—are swayed less by humanitarian concerns and more by geopolitical considerations.

Kashmir and North Korea: Both these regions are tinderboxes, each with the potential to spiral into a much larger conflict. Yet, the UN's approach to them couldn't be more distinct. North Korea, with its nuclear ambitions and defiant posturing, has been at the receiving end of stringent sanctions and widespread international isolation spearheaded by the UN. In contrast, the Kashmir issue, despite its decades-long history and nuclear undertones, remains largely bilateral, with the UN refraining from any substantial intervention. Such differential treatments of equally volatile situations lead many to believe that the UN isn't operating based on a consistent policy or principle. Instead, its actions—or decisions to remain passive—are sculpted by the whims and strategic objectives of major powers.

Latin America: The Backyard Diplomacy

Guatemalan Coup: The 1950s saw the dark shadows of the Cold War stretching across the globe. In its ambit was Guatemala, where a democratically elected government faced the ignominy of being ousted by a coup, allegedly with the backing of the CIA. While such actions, if true, flew in the face of democratic principles and the sovereignty of nations, the UN's response was notably muted. Its silence, for many, wasn't just a failure to act but indicative of a tacit endorsement of Cold War geopolitics, where ideological battles justified meddling in the internal affairs of sovereign nations.

Venezuelan Crisis: As Venezuela descended into a vortex of economic turmoil and political strife, the global community looked on, awaiting decisive international interventions. The UN's response, however, seemed to be on the cooler side of lukewarm. Such tempered reactions, especially when contrasted with the organization's more aggressive postures in other crises, serve as fodder for conspiracy theories. Critics contend that Latin America, often seen as the 'backyard' of the US, is a region where the UN treads lightly, allowing the US to wield disproportionate influence.

This perceived inconsistency fuels beliefs that the UN's actions in the region aren't purely based on a universal set of principles but are influenced by the strategic interests of its dominant member states, especially the US.

In summary, the disparate approaches of the UN across regions—whether borne out of genuine complexities, bias, or major power play—cast shadows over its claim of impartiality. While some inconsistencies might be explained by the nuances of each situation, critics see a pattern that aligns the UN's actions more closely with the interests of global hegemons than with a neutral pursuit of peace and justice.

Through this analysis, the United Nations emerges not as a neutral arbiter but as an entity that is swayed by the interests of dominant powers. Its actions, or the lack thereof, across various global crises hint at an organization that, rather than being an impartial guardian of global peace, might be a tool in the hands of the influential few. As we proceed, the narrative will further dissect the UN's specific initiatives, shedding light on its potential ambitions for a controlled, and possibly dystopian, world order.

Chapter 5
The Push for Digitalization -
Smart Cities, CBDCs, and Digital IDs

Introduction to the Digital Initiatives

The advent of digital technology, marked by the explosion of the internet, artificial intelligence, and interconnected devices, has promised to reshape our world. Pioneering this transformation, the United Nations has positioned itself as a champion of the digital age, envisioning a future where global challenges are addressed through digital solutions. But, beneath this facade of progress, a web of concerns emerges, from privacy invasions to potential centralized control. Could the UN's digital drive be part of a grander design to orchestrate a global digital dictatorship?

Smart Cities: A Closer Look

The allure of smart cities, with their synchronized traffic lights, optimized public transport, and responsive utilities, paints a picture of a futuristic urban utopia. Yet, as we pull back the digital curtain, layers of concern arise, pointing at a potential loss of individuality, privacy, and freedom.

Surveillance State: Beyond the Glossy Facade

The Veil of Efficiency: Modern smart cities promise a future where technology integrates seamlessly into our daily lives, transforming the urban experience. Advanced surveillance systems, fed by a myriad of sensors and cameras, are sold under the banner of efficiency and safety. In these cities, cameras perched on street corners can deter potential criminals, sensors embedded in roads can analyze and divert traffic to prevent congestion, and real-time data analytics can make emergency response swift and precise. On paper, these initiatives present an image of a city that operates like a well-oiled machine, where technology aids in circumventing urban challenges.

However, like all powerful tools, the use or misuse of such extensive surveillance infrastructure largely depends on the intent of those in control. While the direct benefits are undeniable, the potential misuse can have dire consequences.

The Orwellian Fear: As critics rightly point out, there's a thin line between surveillance for safety and surveillance for control. The omnipresence of the State, enabled by this dense web of surveillance, can eerily mirror the dystopian world George Orwell painted in "1984". In such a scenario, the city's infrastructure, instead of serving its residents, could be weaponized against them. With access to vast troves of data, the State could, if it wishes, monitor citizens' activities, preferences, associations, and even predict their actions.

This omnipresent surveillance, even if not actively misused, can have a profound psychological impact on citizens. Knowing that one is constantly being watched could lead to self-censorship. People might refrain from voicing dissenting opinions, attending certain gatherings, or even associating with certain individuals, all out of fear of potential state retribution. The chilling effect on free speech and association could be profound. Moreover, with increasing integration of AI and predictive analytics, there's the fear that individuals could be profiled and potentially penalized for actions they haven't even committed yet, based on predictive behavioral data.

In such a reality, the line between maintaining order and oppressing freedom becomes perilously thin. The trade-off between convenience and privacy, between efficiency and freedom, becomes a central debate. As cities march forward in their quest to become 'smart', it's crucial to ensure that these urban centers remain spaces of freedom, creativity, and dissent, rather than morphing into high-tech cages that monitor and modulate every facet of their residents' lives.

Data Privacy: The Hidden Conundrum

The Digital Gold Rush: In the age of information, data is the new gold. As cities transform into digital hubs, every mundane activity gets logged, processed, and analyzed. Ordering food online, swiping a metro card, using a digital wallet at a local store, or even just walking past a sensor-equipped streetlight—all these actions contribute to an enormous dataset. On one hand, this data can be used to improve urban services, optimize public transport routes, reduce energy consumption, and predict service outages or disruptions. In short, this data can make the city "smarter" and more responsive to its inhabitants' needs.

Yet, there's another side to this digital coin. This vast accumulation of data is not just of interest to urban planners or service providers. Advertisers, corporations, insurance companies, and many other entities can find immense value in this treasure trove of information. Knowing a person's habits, preferences, health conditions, and even social associations can be invaluable for targeted marketing, risk assessment, or other commercial purposes. And herein lies the dilemma—while residents benefit from the conveniences of a digitalized urban environment, they might be unwittingly trading their privacy for comfort.

The Breach Scenario: While proponents of smart cities advocate for the advantages of interconnected urban ecosystems, skeptics highlight a glaring concern: data security. History is replete with instances where even the most secure databases were compromised. From multinational corporations to governmental agencies, no institution has proven to be completely hack-proof.

In the context of smart cities, the potential fallout from a data breach could be catastrophic. Personal information, financial details, health records, and more could be exposed, paving the way for widespread identity theft or even blackmail. But beyond the external threats lie concerns that are even more foundational: What if the very guardians of this data—the city administrators or governments—become the perpetrators? Under the often nebulous umbrella of "national security" or "public interest", governments could access, analyze, and utilize personal data without any substantial oversight or checks and balances. Such unchecked access in the hands of the state could lead to a pervasive surveillance system where citizens' every move is scrutinized, leading to potential misuse, profiling, and discrimination.

In essence, while smart cities bring forth a vision of the future where technology and urban life merge harmoniously, they also present profound ethical, privacy, and security challenges. As the world navigates this new frontier, striking the right balance between leveraging data for public good and safeguarding individual privacy will be paramount. Without adequate safeguards, the dream of smart cities could very well morph into a dystopian nightmare where personal freedoms are sacrificed at the altar of digital progress.

UN's Role: The Orchestrator of the Digital Dream?

Promoting Sustainable Living: The United Nations, as a global entity, has consistently championed sustainable development—a concept that seeks to harmonize the demands of current generations with the need to safeguard the planet for the future. The UN's Sustainable Development Goals (SDGs) are a testament to this commitment, with Goal 11 specifically focusing on making cities inclusive, safe, resilient, and sustainable. Smart cities, with their emphasis on technological solutions to age-old urban problems, naturally align with this vision. By leveraging technology, cities can monitor pollution in real time, manage waste more efficiently, or even reduce energy consumption in public and private spaces. The potential is immense—from using sensors to regulate traffic and reduce congestion, to constructing buildings that are energy neutral. The UN's promotion of such initiatives paints a picture of a future where urban living doesn't come at the planet's expense.

However, this rosy portrayal of tech-driven urban utopias doesn't sit well with everyone. As cities around the globe begin to adopt this model, they're not only sharing technological best practices but also potentially standardizing ways of life, governance structures, and even societal values.

A Global Blueprint: What critics find disconcerting is the notion of a singular, overarching entity—like the UN—having a significant say in shaping the urban landscapes of the future. The question that arises is whether this push towards a digital and sustainable future is merely about conserving resources and enhancing living standards, or if there's more lurking beneath the surface.

Conspiracy theorists and skeptics, often looking beyond the presented narratives, argue that the UN's involvement isn't just altruistic. By setting the blueprint for future cities, the UN, they contend, is positioning itself at the helm of a global transformation. Such a transformation, while ostensibly for "the greater good", could also be leveraged to centralize power, regulate population movements, and monitor citizen activities on an unprecedented scale. The more standardized these smart cities become in their operations and governance, the easier it would be to manage—and potentially control—vast swathes of the global population from a centralized vantage point.

Furthermore, the sheer magnitude of data that smart cities can generate offers a unique tool for governance. While on one hand, this data can be used to enhance public services, on the other, it could also be weaponized to predict, influence, and mold societal behaviors, values, and even ideologies. The UN's potential influence over this vast digital architecture has some worried about the emergence of a monolithic global entity dictating the rhythms of everyday life.

While the promise of smart cities is undeniably tantalizing, it's imperative to tread with caution. The balance between efficiency and freedom, between innovation and surveillance, is a delicate one. The question remains: Is the world ready to navigate this digital maze, and at what cost?

In conclusion, while the UN's involvement in the smart city narrative appears to be rooted in "sustainability and the collective good", there's no denying that such involvement also grants the organization an immense amount of influence. The challenge moving forward will be ensuring that these "Smart Cities" do not come into existence.

CBDCs: The New Age Currency

In the tapestry of human history, the concept of currency has always been fluid, adapting and morphing to fit the socio-political context of its time. Now, as digital technologies pervade every aspect of our lives, our very conception of money is being reinvented. Central Bank Digital Currencies (CBDCs), hailed by some as a revolutionary step in modern finance, are rapidly gaining traction. These digital currencies, in theory, promise to make transactions swifter, reduce financial crime, and bring more people into the formal banking system. However, as we scratch beneath the surface of these promises, the darker implications become more evident, especially when we consider the potential for unchecked control, surveillance, and the power dynamics between the common individual, governing bodies, and global elites.

Control over Transactions: The Double-Edged Sword

A Transparent System: The digitization of currency provides an opportunity to address some of the systemic issues that have plagued traditional finance. Illicit financial activities, including money laundering, terror financing, and tax evasion, have long been challenges that governments and financial institutions grapple with. CBDCs, with their digital nature, can offer a system where transactions are traceable and auditable in real-time. No longer would money be able to flow through the shadows, avoiding the watchful eyes of regulators. Taxes could be levied more efficiently, reducing the burden on honest taxpayers, and ensuring a more equitable distribution of societal resources.

However, the same features that promise transparency and accountability also hold the potential for **unparalleled surveillance**.

Big Brother's Purse Strings: With the advent of CBDCs, every financial transaction, regardless of its size or nature, can be recorded in a digital ledger—a ledger that, theoretically, can be accessed by central banks or even governmental bodies. Such a level of scrutiny is unprecedented. Today, if an individual decides to buy a politically contentious book, donate to a cause that might be frowned upon by the establishment, or simply engage in personal indulgences, these decisions remain private. But in a world dominated by CBDCs, these personal choices are at risk of becoming data points in a vast digital archive, ready to be scrutinized.

Moreover, this raises serious questions about the nature of financial privacy. In societies where political dissent, minority views, or even certain cultural practices are suppressed, the ability of the state to monitor every financial transaction can be a tool of oppression. Could an individual be penalized for financially supporting a cause that goes against the mainstream narrative? Would businesses self-censor, fearing financial repercussions?

The Power to Reverse: One of the foundational principles of traditional banking is the irreversibility of completed transactions. Once money changes hands, only through legal channels or mutual agreement can it be returned. CBDCs, being entirely digital, can potentially change this dynamic. If central authorities possess the technological capability to reverse transactions, it places an enormous amount of power in their hands. A disagreement with a state or central authority could, in theory, lead to financial transactions being nullified.

This level of control can have profound implications. For instance, businesses might find themselves navigating not just commercial challenges, but also the whims and fancies of those in control of the digital currency system. For individuals, it could mean that their financial decisions, rather than being sacrosanct, are perpetually held to scrutiny and potential revision.

In essence, while CBDCs undeniably offer an array of benefits, the ramifications of such a system, especially when controlled by large entities or governments, cannot be ignored. As the world stands on the brink of this new financial frontier, it is imperative to tread with caution, ensuring that the balance of power doesn't tip overwhelmingly in favor of central entities at the expense of individual freedoms and rights.

Financial Exclusion: The Ultimate Leverage

The Dawn of Financial Social Scoring?: While the Chinese Social Credit System seems like a futuristic dystopia to many outside the East, its core principles provide a blueprint for the potential misuse of CBDCs. The system ranks citizens based on their social behavior, punishing those who don't adhere to the state's ideal and rewarding conformists. When this ideology is superimposed onto a financial framework, it paints a grim picture. A CBDC-driven economy could easily integrate such a scoring system. Speak against the ruling class? You might find your digital currency assets dwindling or completely frozen. Attend a protest or voice a controversial opinion? Perhaps, your buying power is reduced, making essential goods and services harder to access. The omnipresence of CBDCs means every transaction, no matter how minor, becomes a potential point of control.

Individual freedoms at Stake: In a society underpinned by CBDCs, personal financial autonomy may become a thing of the past. The overseeing authorities could, at a whim, dictate the very essence of your daily life—where you can buy groceries, which brands you're permitted to support, where your children can go to school, and even which destinations you can visit. Imagine a scenario where a governing body, under the guise of 'national interest', decrees that vacations to a particular country are against the state's ethos. With CBDCs, they could technically prevent transactions related to travel bookings for that destination. Suddenly, your choices and personal freedoms are not just limited; they're defined and restricted by external entities.

Beyond Borders – The Global Ramifications: When delving into the realm of global governance, the United Nations and its myriad economic bodies wield significant influence over member nations. If these organizations were to back specific CBDC protocols or systems, they could inadvertently—or perhaps, intentionally—create a new world order of financial compliance. Countries that refuse to toe the line on certain global mandates might find themselves outcasts in an interconnected digital financial world. This could mean economic sanctions would no longer just be political tools but could be instantaneously executed through digital currency controls, cutting off nations from global trade, aid, and collaboration.

In essence, while the digitalization of currency carries the promise of numerous benefits, it's imperative to consider the broader socio-political implications. The marriage of finance and technology, without adequate checks and balances, could result in an Orwellian reality where personal freedoms are sacrificed at the altar of centralized control and surveillance. As we move towards this new era of finance, it's crucial to approach with caution, lest we inadvertently create a world where the individual becomes but a pawn in a grander game of power and control.

UN's Stance: The Puppeteer in the Shadows?

The United Nations' foray into the realm of digital finance, particularly its stance on Central Bank Digital Currencies (CBDCs), has raised many eyebrows and fueled conspiracy theories. The underlying concerns go beyond the surface-level advantages of CBDCs and delve into the potential for global control and surveillance.

A Digital Financial Vision:

- **Strategic Alignment:** The UN has long championed financial inclusivity and the bridging of the global digital divide. CBDCs align with this broader goal by potentially bringing unbanked populations into the fold of formal financial systems.

- **Global Financial Integration:** The push for CBDCs also signals a move towards more integrated global financial systems. Proponents argue that this could lead to more efficient cross-border transactions and economic stability. However, this raises questions about the loss of financial autonomy for individual nations.

But Why CBDCs?:

- **Central Control vs. Decentralization:** Unlike decentralized cryptocurrencies, which operate independently of a central authority, CBDCs are state-issued and controlled. This centralization is seen by critics as a tool for potential surveillance and control. They argue that the UN's support for CBDCs over decentralized options indicates a preference for systems that can be more easily monitored and regulated at a global level.

- **Global Agenda Compliance:** The preference for CBDCs is perceived by some as a method to enforce compliance with global financial policies and agendas. With digital currencies, international bodies could have more leverage over national economies, potentially influencing domestic policy decisions through financial mechanisms.

Consolidation of Financial Power:

- **Global Policy Influence:** The widespread adoption of CBDCs could result in global entities like the UN or the IMF having unprecedented influence over individual financial transactions. This consolidation of financial power might allow these entities to enact and enforce global economic policies directly, bypassing national governments.

- **Potential for Economic Homogenization:** This scenario could lead to a homogenization of global economic policies, where diverse economic models and practices are supplanted by a standardized, one-size-fits-all approach. Critics argue this could erode national economic sovereignty and exacerbate existing economic inequalities.

- **Privacy and Surveillance Concerns:** The shift to a digitally centralized currency system intensifies concerns about privacy and data security. The ability to track and monitor financial transactions on a global scale presents a potential Orwellian scenario, where individual financial freedom is compromised in the name of global economic stability and security.

In conclusion, the UN's advocacy for CBDCs, while ostensibly aimed at promoting financial inclusivity and global economic integration, is viewed by critics as a step towards a more controlled and monitored financial system. This development raises profound questions about the balance between global economic cooperation and national sovereignty, as well as individual financial privacy and autonomy.

The journey of CBDCs, from a financial innovation to a potential tool of control, is a testament to the complexities of the digital age. While the efficiencies are evident, the implications on personal freedom and global power dynamics remain a deeply debated concern. The world stands on the cusp of a financial revolution, and its trajectory could redefine the essence of money and power.

Digital IDs: The Identity of the Future

Single Point of Failure: The Achilles' Heel of Digital IDs

As the United Nations and various international entities advocate for the integration of Digital IDs, the perceived benefits of streamlined verification and enhanced security come with their own set of significant risks. This centralization of personal data poses a unique challenge to privacy, security, and individual autonomy, raising serious ethical and practical concerns.

A Unified Database:

- **Complete Personal Dossier:** The concept of a Digital ID involves amalgamating an individual's complete personal data spectrum into a single digital entity. This concentration of personal information – ranging from biometrics to personal preferences – could be unprecedented in its scope and depth.

- **Potential for Abuse:** This unification raises the specter of abuse. In the hands of a governing body, such detailed personal profiles could be used for extensive monitoring and controlling the populace. The possibility of a 'Big Brother' scenario, where the line between governance and surveillance blurs, becomes a real concern.

The Hacker's Paradise:

- **Cybersecurity Vulnerabilities:** A centralized digital identity system represents a highly attractive target for cybercriminals. A successful breach could compromise the personal data of millions, if not billions, of individuals at once. The fallout from such a breach would be catastrophic, affecting every aspect of a person's life.

- **Insider Threats:** The threat is not just external. The system's very nature could make it susceptible to exploitation from within by corrupt officials or employees, who might access and manipulate data for personal or political reasons.

Irrevocable Errors:

- **Systemic Glitches and Errors:** The reliance on technology means that any systemic error could have widespread and possibly irreversible consequences. An error could lead to misidentification, wrongful exclusion from services, or unjust persecution.

- **Difficulty in Rectification:** Rectifying errors in a digital identity system could be a complex, time-consuming process. Individuals might find themselves entangled in bureaucratic red tape to prove their identity or rectify inaccuracies, leading to loss of access to critical services and rights.

In summary, while Digital IDs promise efficiency and security, they also bring forth the risks of centralization, making individuals vulnerable to both external and internal threats. The transition to such a system demands rigorous scrutiny and robust safeguards to protect individual rights and freedoms. The challenges posed by Digital IDs highlight a crucial debate in the modern world – the trade-off between convenience and privacy, security and freedom.

Tool of Suppression: The Orwellian Fear

Digital IDs, while ostensibly designed for streamlining identity verification, hold the potential to morph into instruments of surveillance and control. This transformation from a facilitative tool to a mechanism of suppression represents a grave threat to civil liberties and democratic freedoms.

Beyond Verification:

- **Predictive Policing and Social Sorting:** With an extensive database, authorities could employ Digital IDs for purposes well beyond basic identification. Advanced analytics could enable predictive policing or social sorting, where individuals are categorized and treated differently based on their data profiles. This could lead to a society where personal choices and behaviors are constantly scrutinized and judged against opaque standards.

- **Behavioral Manipulation:** The data amassed through Digital IDs could be used to subtly influence behavior. From nudging citizens towards certain governmental agendas to penalizing those who deviate from prescribed norms, the scope for manipulation is vast and troubling.

A Tool Against Dissent:

- **Surveillance State:** In an authoritarian setting, Digital IDs could transform into a powerful surveillance tool. They could be used to monitor citizens' movements, associations, and even their participation in political activities. Such surveillance could stifle dissent, discourage activism, and entrench the power of the ruling elite.

- **Selective Service Denial:** Governments could leverage Digital IDs to selectively deny services or rights to those deemed 'undesirable' or 'non-compliant'. Access to banking, healthcare, or travel could become contingent on one's conformity to state mandates, effectively coercing compliance through systemic exclusion.

The End of Anonymity:

- **Eroding Safe Spaces:** The erosion of anonymity could have chilling effects on political discourse and activism. Whistleblowers, political dissidents, or even ordinary citizens who wish to voice concerns anonymously would find themselves exposed and vulnerable.

- **Digital Footprints as Evidence:** The digital footprints left via Digital IDs could be used as evidence against individuals in a manner that circumvents traditional legal protections. The mere act of visiting certain websites or communicating with certain individuals could be misconstrued or used to incriminate.

In summary, the implementation of Digital IDs harbors risks that extend far beyond issues of data security. They pose a fundamental threat to the tenets of privacy, freedom of expression, and democratic engagement. Their potential to be exploited as tools of suppression and control necessitates a critical examination of their broader implications, ensuring that the march towards digitalization does not trample over the foundational values of a free and open society.

UN's Advocacy: A Global Push with Hidden Agendas?

The Allure of ID2020: At the heart of the United Nation's digital push is the ID2020 initiative. On paper, its objectives appear noble. Over a billion individuals globally lack any form of official identification, rendering them invisible in the eyes of bureaucracy and locking them out of essential services. ID2020 seeks to bridge this chasm, leveraging digital technologies to provide a form of identity to the disenfranchised.

Advocates believe this can be a game-changer, heralding financial inclusion and optimizing service delivery, from healthcare to education.

But Why The Push?: However, the velocity and intensity with which the United Nations is propelling this initiative has raised eyebrows. Detractors and skeptics raise pertinent questions about the underlying motivations. Why is there such a fervor to digitize identity on a global scale? The dark underbelly of conspiracy theories speculates about a more sinister, globalist plot. Proponents of these theories often warn of an overarching design to consolidate control over humanity, curbing freedoms and sovereignty. In this speculative scenario, digital identities are not mere tools for inclusivity but the foundation blocks of a monolithic global governance model.

A Future Without Privacy?: The United Nations, in its global advocacy role, wields considerable influence over member nations. Their endorsement of an initiative like ID2020 isn't merely symbolic; it can profoundly shape policies and decision-making across borders. This confluence of global mandates and national policies stirs apprehensions. As the UN steers the ship, there's growing anxiety that individual nations may relinquish their unique cultural, social, and political contexts. The result? A standardized, global approach to digital identity that disregards local intricacies. This not only erases the rich tapestry of global diversity but also augments concerns over privacy and personal freedom. The individual, in such a landscape, may become but a digit in a vast global database, their identity, behaviors, and choices under perpetual scrutiny.

In summary, while the path of digital transformation, especially in the realm of finance and identity, promises a myriad of advancements, it's essential to tread with caution. The convergence of technology, power, and global influence, if left unchecked, could alter the very essence of personal freedom, autonomy, and the cherished tenets of individual sovereignty. As we navigate this brave new world, the lines etched by

George Orwell in '1984' serve as a stark reminder, "Big Brother is watching you."

The debate surrounding Digital IDs is emblematic of the larger discourse about the digital age. As technology continues to permeate every aspect of our lives, the balance between convenience and privacy, between security and freedom, becomes all the more precarious. The Digital ID conundrum, then, isn't just about identity but about the kind of future we're paving for ourselves.

The Overarching Narrative

The narrative around the UN's involvement in digital initiatives carries both explicit and implicit messages. Proponents (people that will gain from it) argue that these projects represent steps toward addressing global challenges. Yet, there's a huge counter-narrative suggesting that the actual aims are much more strategic and sinister.

Benevolence or Ulterior Motive? From the outset, the United Nations' technological endeavors gleam with a promise. They seem to herald an age of unbridled progress where the digital divide narrows, and inclusivity is not just a buzzword but a tangible reality. The UN portrays itself as a harbinger of change, tapping into technology's vast potential to redress longstanding global challenges. Yet, amidst these glowing prospects, a shadow of doubt looms large. Detractors contend that beneath this façade of benevolence lurks a more calculated strategy. The question arises - are these digital initiatives sincere efforts towards a brighter future or sophisticated instruments of control, adroitly masqueraded as global altruism?

The Panopticon Effect: Jeremy Bentham's conceptual design, the Panopticon, serves as a haunting metaphor in today's digital age. A structure where inhabitants are under constant potential surveillance, the Panopticon's principles mirror the fears of a world where privacy is a mere relic of the past. The United Nations' fervent push for digital projects has, unintentionally or otherwise, exacerbated these fears. Critics postulate that the UN is not merely championing technological advancements but rather curating a global landscape where omnipresent observation is the norm. In such a world, one's every move, utterance, and financial transaction is subject to scrutiny — a chilling reality where the observer remains unseen, but their presence is ubiquitously felt.

The Loss of Autonomy: The digital realm, by its very nature, thrives on connectivity. But as the tendrils of this interconnected matrix grow, they bind not just machines but humans as well. There's an undeniable allure to a world where everything is interlinked, offering unprecedented levels of convenience and efficiency. Yet, this very interlinking poses existential questions. As individuals become mere nodes in this vast network, what becomes of personal agency? The specter of a future where autonomy is sacrificed at the altar of digitalization looms large. The more enmeshed we become in this digital web, the greater the risk of eroding the very essence of individuality, freedom, and perhaps, our core humanity.

In weaving the story of the UN's digital initiatives, we are confronted with a mosaic of conflicting narratives. While the promise of a technologically enriched future beckons, the concerns of overarching control and diminishing personal freedom cast long, dark shadows. The interplay between these contrasting tales will shape not only the future of digitalization but the very fabric of our global society.

Conclusion of the Chapter

The voyage into the digital age, while promising unprecedented advancements, beckons with it a Pandora's box of challenges and dilemmas. This chapter's journey into the intricate tapestry of the UN's digital endeavors offers both a glimpse of hope and cautionary tales.

The Double-Edged Nature of Digitalization: In an age where speed, efficiency, and convenience are often hailed as the benchmarks of progress, digitalization stands as a towering testament to human ingenuity. Its potential to transform economies, bridge divides, and render services at a pace once deemed impossible is undeniable. Yet, like all tools wielded by humankind, it's not devoid of its pitfalls. The same systems that promise seamless global connectivity and swift transactions also harbor the potential to become tools of surveillance, eroding the sanctity of individual privacy. Moreover, the digital realm, despite its veneer of invulnerability, remains susceptible to threats. Cyberattacks, data breaches, and the perennial fear of extensive power outages underline the vulnerabilities of an over-reliant digital world. It paints a grim picture where, in the wake of a significant technological disruption, societies could come to a standstill, rendering basic services and essential mechanisms inoperative.

A Choice for Humanity: As humanity teeters on the brink of this digital epoch, profound introspection is warranted. The allure of a world envisioned by the UN, where digital solutions seemingly rectify longstanding issues, is tempting. However, is this vision one of authentic altruism or a calculated orchestration with ulterior motives? The call of the hour isn't mere adoption but discernment. Before plunging headfirst into this digital abyss, society must weigh the pros and cons, ensuring that the digital realm we cultivate remains rooted in the tenets of human dignity, liberty, and equity.

In Whose Hands Does the Future Lie? The tapestry of the future is being woven with threads of technology, and those who hold these threads command an influence that's both awe-inspiring and disconcerting. As digital mediums permeate every facet of existence, the discourse around control becomes paramount. If there's even an iota of veracity in the whispers suggesting the UN's aspirations for digital dominance, the global populace cannot remain passive spectators. The future, especially one so intrinsically tied to technology, should not be the exclusive domain of a select few, irrespective of their stature or intent. It becomes a clarion call for civil society, technologists, policymakers, and every stakeholder to partake in this discourse, ensuring that the digital age, in all its glory and peril, remains an era for the many, not the few.

In the wake of rapid technological advancements, the world stands at a crossroads. While the promises of a digital utopia beckon, shadows of a controlled, monitored, and homogenized global society loom large. Only by understanding, debating, and critically examining these developments can we hope to steer our shared destiny in a direction that celebrates humanity in all its diversity and freedom.

In conclusion, as the pages of this chapter fold, they leave behind more questions than answers. The odyssey into the digital realm is as much about technology as it is about the very essence of humanity. The choices made today will echo in the annals of history, shaping not just the future of technology but the destiny of humankind itself.

Chapter 6
The SDG Plan: A Deep Dive

<u>The SDG Plan: A Deep Dive</u>

The United Nations, for decades, has been at the forefront of formulating global agendas that ostensibly seek to address the world's most pressing issues. The Sustainable Development Goals (SDGs) serve as the most recent testament to this endeavor. But like all grand narratives, there's more to the SDGs than meets the eye.

Origins of the SDGs: The transition from the Millennium Development Goals (MDGs) to the Sustainable Development Goals (SDGs) marked a significant shift in the UN's approach to global challenges. While the MDGs, initiated at the dawn of the new millennium, were primarily focused on alleviating extreme poverty and related challenges in developing nations, the SDGs projected a broader, more ambitious vision. Launched amid much fanfare in September 2015 at the UN General Assembly, the SDGs were introduced as the next logical step in the global developmental journey.

Presented as a universal clarion call, the SDGs ambitiously sought to provide a comprehensive roadmap to a better future — a world devoid of poverty, a planet restored and protected, and an environment where every individual could enjoy the fruits of peace and prosperity by the year 2030. At first glance, the sheer audacity of these goals would make one laud the UN for its visionary outlook.

However, the magnitude and the all-encompassing nature of these goals also raise eyebrows. The skeptic's perspective questions whether such lofty ideals, irrespective of their noble intent, could become instruments of overarching control.

Beneath the surface of these noble goals lies a more intricate web. The SDGs, in their essence, are not merely aspirational objectives. They represent a highly detailed and systematic approach to global governance. By setting standards on virtually every facet of human existence, from health and education to economic growth and environmental protection, the SDGs have a reach that's unparalleled in history.

This expansive influence inherently offers the UN an unprecedented leverage over nations, regions, and communities. When goals are so vast and universal, they can be employed as benchmarks to judge and potentially intervene in the internal matters of sovereign states. With the SDGs, the UN isn't merely suggesting a path to progress; it's prescribing a specific route, a standardized vision of development that might not always align with local contexts, cultural nuances, and individual nation's aspirations.

Furthermore, while the SDGs speak of prosperity, peace, and planet, they seldom delve into the specifics of ensuring individual freedoms, sovereignty, and cultural preservation. Such an ambitious framework, designed to impact every aspect of life on Earth, might seem altruistic on the exterior. Yet, it can also be perceived as a meticulous blueprint for global dominance, subtly dictating the pace, direction, and nature of development across the globe.

In conclusion, the SDGs, while groundbreaking in their scope and intent, warrant a more in-depth scrutiny. As the world navigates the complexities of the 21st century, understanding the true implications, both overt and covert, of such grand global narratives becomes imperative. While the promise of a better world is alluring, it's essential to determine at what cost and under whose terms this "better" world is being constructed.

Overview of the 17 Goals:

The United Nations, in its quest for global betterment, set forth the Sustainable Development Goals (SDGs) in 2015. Seventeen in number, these goals seek to address a vast range of challenges, from the pangs of poverty to the perils of climate change. The year 2030 was marked as the horizon, a deadline for the world to achieve these objectives. But, as with every silver lining, there's often a cloud casting shadows, and the SDGs aren't immune to skeptical examination.

1. No Poverty:

Official Narrative: A brighter future, free from the debilitating grip of poverty, is envisioned as the ultimate aim. The goal seeks to uplift those in destitution, providing every human being with resources and opportunities to lead a life of dignity.

Most Likely Outcome: Critics assert that the true intent behind this goal is not to eradicate poverty but to centralize control over global resources. They argue that under the pretext of poverty reduction, global elites will orchestrate the distribution of resources in a manner that tightens their grip on wealth and power. This will lead to a scenario where, instead of facilitating equitable resource distribution, poverty eradication becomes a tool for consolidating wealth, creating a vast economic chasm between the global elite and the masses. The skepticism is rooted in the belief that what is presented as a noble pursuit will actually serve to further entrench economic disparities.

2. Zero Hunger:

Official Narrative: At the heart of this goal lies the vision of a well-fed world. A realm where hunger is a relic of the past, and every individual, regardless of where they reside, has access to nutritious food throughout the year.

Most Likely Outcome: The true implications of a world without hunger go beyond the superficial goal of feeding the hungry. This objective, in reality, will lead to a world where a few dominant corporations control what and how people eat. The push towards zero hunger will inevitably pivot towards an increased reliance on genetically modified foods, controlled by corporate patents. This shift would not just address hunger but will also strategically position these corporations to have undue control over global food sources. Consequently, the goal of eliminating hunger will become a facade for establishing a monopolistic grip on food, making nations and their populations dependent on a handful of entities. This concentration of power will undermine national sovereignty and grant a few corporations unparalleled power over one of the most fundamental aspects of human survival – the food supply.

3. **Good Health and Well-being:**

   Official Narrative: The vision for this goal is a world where every individual, irrespective of age, enjoys the boon of good health and overall well-being. This paints an idyllic scenario where health crises are efficiently managed and where medical advancements are accessible to all.

   Most Likely Outcome: The global promotion of this goal will likely serve as a gateway to a centralized, globalized healthcare system, heavily influenced by major international pharmaceutical corporations. Under the guise of ensuring good health and well-being for all, nations will become increasingly dependent on these conglomerates for healthcare policies and medical supplies. This shift will centralize crucial healthcare decisions, placing them in the hands of a few global entities, effectively overriding local expertise and understanding of regional health needs. The result will be a healthcare landscape where priorities and decisions are dictated by these powerful entities, transforming healthcare from a local and personalized service into a one-size-fits-all model controlled by the highest global bidders.

4. Quality Education:

Official Narrative: Education, they say, is the cornerstone of progress. The UN, through this goal, aspires for a world where every individual, regardless of their circumstances, has access to quality education that empowers them for the future.

Most Likely Outcome: The globalized education system the UN aims for will lead to a uniform, one-size-fits-all curriculum. This approach will erase the rich diversity of cultural and regional perspectives, replacing them with a standardized, homogenized narrative controlled by global elites. Instead of nurturing critical and independent thinkers, this system will churn out individuals molded to fit a singular global perspective (sheep). The consequence will be a loss of educational diversity and the suppression of individual thought, as education becomes a tool for global conformity rather than a means of personal and cultural development.

5. Gender Equality:

Official Narrative: At the heart of this goal lies the empowerment of every woman and girl on the planet. A world where gender is no longer a barrier to opportunities and where every woman stands tall, their rights and aspirations recognized and protected.

Most Likely Outcome: The global push for gender equality will disrupt traditional societal structures that are deeply ingrained in the cultural and historical fabric of many societies. These structures often provide stability and continuity. Enforcing global standards of gender equality will rapidly alter these societal dynamics, leading to societal rifts and potential unrest. The pursuit of gender equality, as dictated by the UN, will not just challenge but potentially unravel these traditional systems, undermining the social balance and causing widespread destabilization. This approach neglects the complexities and diversities of cultural interpretations of gender roles, imposing a one-dimensional view of equality that may not align with local values and practices.

6. Clean Water and Sanitation:

Official Narrative: At its core, this goal envisions a world where every individual, regardless of where they reside, has unimpeded access to clean water and sanitation. This taps into the universal understanding that water is life, and ensuring its purity and availability is foundational for human existence and progress.

Most Likely Outcome: The pursuit of this goal will likely lead to the privatization and commodification of water resources. Control over water - a critical life-sustaining resource - will shift from being a communal right to a privately owned commodity. Access to clean water will become a matter of financial ability rather than a basic human right. This shift will disproportionately impact lower-income communities and developing countries, exacerbating inequalities. Corporations and private entities will increasingly dominate water management, and their profit motives may override the essential human need for water, leading to scenarios where people are denied access due to inability to pay.

7. Affordable and Clean Energy:

Official Narrative: The promise of this goal is a world powered by clean, sustainable energy, available and affordable to all. This paints a future where the environment is respected, and our energy sources are in harmony with the planet.

Most Likely Outcome: The shift to clean energy will likely result in the monopolization of energy sources by large international conglomerates. This concentration of power will allow these entities to dictate terms, manipulate energy prices, and control supply chains. Nations, particularly those with developing economies, will become heavily reliant on these corporations for their energy needs. This dependency will create imbalances in global power dynamics, with the potential for exploitation and economic coercion by these energy giants. The promise of affordable and clean energy will be overshadowed by the reality of a few corporations holding sway over the world's energy resources.

8. Decent Work and Economic Growth:

Official Narrative: Economic growth, when inclusive and sustainable, can elevate societies, providing employment opportunities and improving living standards for all. This goal sets forth a vision where economic progress is harmonized with social needs.

Most Likely Outcome: The drive for universal economic growth will likely result in increased corporatization and market monopolization by global entities. This will erode the economic autonomy of individual nations, as major corporations will dominate job markets and dictate employment standards, wages, and work policies. Local businesses and entrepreneurs will struggle to compete, leading to a loss of diversity in the marketplace and a concentration of economic power in the hands of a few multinational corporations. These developments will ultimately undermine the goal of inclusive growth, favoring corporate interests over the welfare of the global workforce.

9. **Industry, Innovation, and Infrastructure:**

   Official Narrative: A future envisaged where modern infrastructure paves the way for resilient societies, and innovation is the cornerstone of progress. By enhancing the foundation of our industries and spurring creative solutions, the goal is to boost economies and improve living conditions.

   Most Likely Outcome: The intertwining of industry with innovation will likely lead to the domination of multinational corporations in local markets, overshadowing and potentially displacing local businesses. As technology advances rapidly, there is an increased risk of technological surveillance. In an increasingly digital world, data becomes a highly sought-after commodity, and with corporations gaining vast access to this data, there is a significant potential for its misuse. This could result in violations of individual privacy and freedoms, as personal data could be exploited for corporate gain or manipulated to influence consumer behavior and societal norms.

10. **Reduced Inequality:**

   Official Narrative: A call to bridge the chasm between the haves and the have-nots, both within countries and among them. By leveling the playing field, the vision is to ensure that opportunities and resources are available to all, irrespective of their socio-economic or geographical standing.

   Most Likely Outcome: The attempt to reduce inequality on a global scale will likely serve as a means for power centralization. If global organizations like the UN begin to control and set standards for equitable distribution, this will lead to an excessive aggregation of power. Rather than truly empowering the less privileged, it will transform into a method to impose terms on sovereign nations, under the pretense of fostering equality. This could result in a top-down approach where decisions and policies are dictated by a global elite, potentially ignoring or overriding the specific needs, contexts, and voices of individual nations and communities.

11. Sustainable Cities and Communities:

Official Narrative: The future city is painted as a hub of inclusivity, safety, and sustainability. With the urban population swelling, the emphasis is on developing cities that can cater to their citizens while respecting the environment.

Most Likely Outcome: The development of sustainable urban centers will inevitably lead to increased surveillance and a loss of individual privacy. Smart cities, replete with advanced technologies like sensors and cameras, will ensure that citizens are constantly monitored. Such omnipresent surveillance will erode the sense of personal space and freedom. Moreover, the dominance of global architectural and design firms in shaping these urban spaces will likely result in the diminishing of local architectural practices and cultural identities. Cities around the world may start to lose their unique character, giving way to a homogenized, global urban culture that prioritizes efficiency and sustainability over historical and cultural preservation.

12. Responsible Consumption and Production:

Official Narrative: A vision is painted of a world where societies realize the implications of overconsumption and wastage, leading to a global shift towards more sustainable consumption and production patterns. The emphasis here is on optimizing resource use, reducing waste, and promoting sustainable practices at all stages of the production chain.

Most Likely Outcome: This goal will likely lead to stringent regulations and control over individual consumption behaviors.

Governing bodies will define what constitutes "responsible consumption," and these standards will heavily dictate personal choices. From dietary habits to purchasing decisions, individuals will find their freedoms increasingly curtailed in the name of sustainability. Such regulations, while well-intentioned, will infringe upon personal autonomy, transforming individual lifestyle choices into regulated actions driven by global sustainability mandates. This could create a scenario where personal agency is sacrificed at the altar of global environmental goals, leading to widespread discontent and a feeling of loss of control over one's own life choices.

13. Climate Action:

Official Narrative: With the looming threat of climate change, the world is called upon to take proactive and decisive action to mitigate the impacts of global warming. Through collaborative efforts, nations are urged to adopt sustainable practices, invest in green technologies, and reduce carbon footprints.

Most Likely Outcome: The implementation of climate action measures will disproportionately impact developing countries. These nations, already grappling with economic challenges, will be subject to strict environmental regulations that will significantly hinder their industrial growth and economic development. Developed countries, which historically contributed the most to carbon emissions, will impose these restrictions, perpetuating a cycle of economic inequality. The measures, though aimed at environmental conservation, will create an uneven playing field, where the burden of climate action falls heavily on those less responsible for the crisis. This imbalance will not only hamper the growth of developing economies but also deepen global economic disparities, leading to increased tension and potential conflicts between developed and developing nations.

14. Life Below Water:

Official Narrative: The vast oceans and marine resources that cover our planet are invaluable. Recognizing this, the goal aims to protect marine life, reduce pollution, and ensure that the utilization of marine resources is sustainable and does not endanger the rich biodiversity of our oceans.

Most Likely Outcome: The enforcement of sustainable practices for marine conservation will inevitably lead to geopolitical tensions over ocean resources and territories. Nations with extensive maritime boundaries will engage in disputes over fishing rights, access to marine resources, and control of territorial waters. These conflicts will be exacerbated as countries attempt to assert their dominance or protect their interests in rich marine areas. Moreover, the implementation of international marine conservation laws may lead to restrictions that disproportionately affect smaller, less powerful nations dependent on marine resources for their livelihoods. Consequently, these countries will struggle to balance environmental commitments with the economic needs of their coastal communities, leading to a rise in local and regional tensions.

15. Life on Land:

Official Narrative: The lush forests, expansive grasslands, and myriad ecosystems on land harbor the majority of Earth's biodiversity. Recognizing the importance of terrestrial ecosystems, this goal seeks to combat desertification, restore degraded lands, and ensure the sustainable use of terrestrial resources.

Most Likely Outcome: In pursuing these objectives, national sovereignty and the rights of local communities, particularly indigenous groups, will be significantly challenged. Global directives aimed at conserving terrestrial ecosystems will impose stringent land usage restrictions, leading to conflicts between traditional practices and new regulations. Indigenous communities, who have historically maintained a harmonious relationship with their land, will face disruption in their way of life. Governments will struggle to balance the demands of global sustainability against the needs and rights of their citizens. This approach will likely erode the autonomy of nations over their natural resources, potentially leading to social unrest and resistance against perceived external control.

16. Peace, Justice, and Strong Institutions:

Official Narrative: The foundation of any progressive society is peace and justice. This goal underscores the importance of reducing violence, ending abuse, and establishing transparent institutions that are accountable to the masses.

Most Likely Outcome: The pursuit of universal peace and justice will lead to the establishment of a centralized global governing body, overshadowing and potentially undermining national judicial systems. This will erode the diversity and uniqueness of judicial systems shaped by cultural and historical contexts. The drive for a homogenized form of governance, under the guise of achieving global peace and justice, will diminish the sovereignty of individual nations and their ability to administer justice as per their societal norms. This will result in a standardized, one-size-fits-all approach to law and governance, potentially conflicting with local values and practices and leading to widespread discontent among nations striving to preserve their judicial independence.

17. Partnerships for the Goals:

Official Narrative: Recognizing that the challenges faced by humanity are intricate and interconnected, this goal promotes global collaboration and partnerships. By working together, nations can pool resources, knowledge, and expertise to realize the vision set by the SDGs.

Most Likely Outcome: The push for global partnerships will lead to alliances that centralize power in the hands of a few global elites, diminishing the influence and autonomy of individual nations. Under the guise of collaboration, major players will dictate terms, reducing smaller and less influential nations to passive roles in global decision-making. This power imbalance will result in the interests of the few being prioritized over the many, undermining the concept of equitable and genuine partnership. The global collaboration envisaged will be overshadowed by a hierarchical structure where decision-making is controlled by a select group, compromising the democratic essence of true partnership and cooperation.

In conclusion, the Sustainable Development Goals, while ostensibly heralding an era of global progress and unity, need a more critical examination. Beneath their utopian veneer lies a complex web of potential consequences that would reshape the world order in ways that are deeply concerning. It's crucial to recognize that these goals, while noble in intent, are vehicles for centralizing power, undermining national sovereignty, and eroding individual rights under the guise of global betterment. The pursuit of these objectives, if not carefully scrutinized and balanced, will lead to the dominance of a select elite, dictating global norms and priorities at the expense of local needs and diversities. Therefore, it's the collective responsibility of the global community to dissect, debate, and, where necessary, challenge the trajectory of these goals to ensure that the journey towards a better world does not sacrifice the very principles of democracy, freedom, and self-determination it aims to uphold. The path forward must be navigated with both hope and a keen awareness of the potential pitfalls that accompany any grand vision of global transformation.

Intent vs. Reality

At face value, the SDGs champion a harmonious global vision. Yet, beneath this glossy veneer, critics and conspiracy theorists argue that there are hidden agendas that would compromise national sovereignty, individual freedoms, cultural identities, and the critics would be right.

Standardization vs. Individuality:

Altruistic Intent: At its core, the idea of having a standardized set of goals is rooted in the aspiration to have a common roadmap. By ensuring all nations are on the same page, the hope is to foster a spirit of global cooperation, wherein nations support and uplift one another, driving collective progress towards universally agreed-upon benchmarks.

Underlying Concerns:

However, beneath this well-intentioned plan lie a multitude of concerns, some of which are:

- **Homogenization of Cultures:** The tapestry of human civilization is rich and diverse, woven with myriad cultural threads that span histories, geographies, and philosophies. A singular framework, while aiming for unity, could inadvertently result in the erosion of this diversity. Adopting a "one-size-fits-all" approach might push nations to forsake their unique identities, traditions, and values, leading to a globalized society that lacks the vibrant mosaic of various cultures. This homogenization not only results in the loss of cultural heritage but also threatens the preservation of indigenous knowledge and practices that have been passed down for generations.

- **Suppression of Minority Rights:** In the race to achieve these global standards, there lies the danger of sidelining minority voices. As nations scramble to fit into this new mold, the interests of smaller ethnic, linguistic, or cultural groups could be trampled upon. These groups, already marginalized in many societies, might find themselves further ostracized, their needs and concerns deprioritized in favor of larger national or global agendas. Such suppression can lead to social unrest, exacerbate inequalities, and endanger the very fabric of societies.

- **Loss of National Autonomy:** The idea of sovereign nations is predicated on the belief that each country knows what's best for its people. However, the imposition of a global standard can challenge this notion. Nations might find themselves in predicaments where the global directive is at odds with their national interests, values, or the collective will of their people. Adjusting national policies to suit these global goals could mean compromising on home-grown strategies that cater specifically to the unique challenges and aspirations of a country's populace. This might sow seeds of discontent, as citizens feel their government's actions are being directed not by their own needs but by an external global agenda.

Economic Control:

Altruistic Intent: The vision is clear: a world where resources are optimally utilized, where economies are interconnected, and where nations pull each other up, ensuring that the fruits of progress are enjoyed by all, not just a privileged few. Such interconnectedness promises reduced economic disparities, particularly between the global North and the global South.

Underlying Concerns:

Despite the seemingly benign intent, the path to such interconnectedness is fraught with challenges and concerns:

- **Dependency on International Entities:** International monetary bodies, like the International Monetary Fund (IMF) or the World Bank, while originally established to provide financial assistance and policy advice, have often been accused of wielding undue influence. Countries, particularly those in the developing world, could find themselves in a precarious position where accepting financial aid comes with strings attached. These "strings" often manifest as policy directives or reforms that might not align with the nation's ground realities or cultural nuances. Such influence, therefore, runs the risk of turning sovereign nations into quasi-client states, with their economic policies being shaped not by the will of their people, but by the agendas of these international entities.

- **Restrictive Trade Agreements:** Trade agreements, in theory, should be mutually beneficial contracts between nations, fostering economic cooperation and growth. However, in the shadow of global goals, there is a potential for power imbalances. Nations, in their zeal to meet certain benchmarks or to gain access to resources or markets, might be pushed into agreements that are skewed against them. Such agreements could compromise national interests, limit economic autonomy, and trap nations in unfavorable conditions that hamper their long-term economic prospects.

- **Overreach of Multinational Corporations:** The global economic landscape is increasingly dominated by multinational corporations. While these entities can bring in investment, technology, and jobs, there's a darker side to this coin. A globalized economic platform might amplify the power of these corporations, allowing them to gain monopolistic or oligopolistic control over local markets. This can lead to a myriad of issues: from stifling local innovation and entrepreneurship to exerting undue influence over national policies. Furthermore, with their vast resources, these corporations can overshadow local businesses, leading to economic homogenization and potentially undermining the cultural and economic fabric of local communities.

In summation, while the pursuit of global economic collaboration is commendable, it's imperative to be wary of the undercurrents of power and influence. The ideal of global economic prosperity shouldn't morph into a landscape where nations lose their economic agency, and local businesses are overshadowed by global giants.

Surveillance and Monitoring:

Altruistic Intent: In a complex world, tracking progress towards such ambitious goals as the SDGs is no easy task. To paint an accurate picture of global development and needs, collecting data from nations becomes imperative. This isn't just a matter of ticking off boxes; it's about understanding where efforts are yielding results and where more attention is required. It's about ensuring that no nation or community is left behind in the march towards a better future.

Underlying Concerns:

However, with great data comes great responsibility—and the potential for misuse:

- **Invasion of Privacy:** To meet the vast and varied metrics of the SDGs, a significant amount of data is required. While some of this data is macroeconomic or demographic in nature, a lot can be deeply personal. Think health records indicating a person's illnesses, or financial records that shed light on an individual's economic standing. In a digital age defined by concerns over privacy, the idea that such personal data could be accessed, shared, or analyzed by international entities is alarming. It raises ethical questions about the boundaries of surveillance and the sanctity of individual privacy.

- **Manipulation of Data:** Data, while often hailed as objective, is subject to manipulation. Whether it's nations wanting to present themselves in a more positive light, or entities looking to leverage skewed data for aid, resources, or political favor, the potential for data manipulation cannot be ignored. Such manipulation not only undermines the authenticity and trust in the SDG monitoring process but could also lead to misallocation of resources or misguided policies.

- **Centralized Data Repositories:** The idea of centralized databases, housing information from all corners of the globe, is both a logistical solution and a potential nightmare. On one hand, such repositories can be hubs of knowledge, aiding in swift and efficient data analysis. On the other, they become glaring targets. In a world where cyber warfare and espionage are real threats, these databases could be prime targets for hacking, sabotage, or illicit information extraction.

While the SDGs present a hopeful vision for the future, it's crucial to discern between their stated objectives and the potential real-world implications of their implementation. The endeavor to sculpt a globally unified future might come at the cost of the diverse tapestry that makes our world rich and unique. As with all global initiatives, it's imperative to tread with caution, ensuring that the path to a better tomorrow doesn't inadvertently pave the way for a compromised today.

To sum up, while data-driven insights are pivotal for the success of the SDGs, it's crucial to tread with caution. The ethical implications of surveillance, the potential pitfalls of data manipulation, and the cyber risks associated with centralized databases are all concerns that need serious contemplation. In a quest to build a better world, it's essential to ensure that foundational principles of privacy, integrity, and security aren't compromised.

Critical Examination

The Sustainable Development Goals (SDGs) might appear as an admirable roadmap to global prosperity. However, when critically examined, certain aspects raise flags and stoke concerns about their true intentions and possible repercussions.

Vagueness and Ambiguity

Concern: The SDGs, for all their promise, are often framed in terms that are both broad and generalized. Such framing, while allowing flexibility, opens doors for manipulation and misrepresentation.

In-Depth Examination:

- **Interpretative Leeway:** Language, by its nature, is open to interpretation. However, in the realm of global policy and action, the stakes for such interpretations are incredibly high. Consider terms like "Decent Work" or "Quality Education." At face value, they seem universally positive, but the devil, as always, is in the details. For instance, what one nation considers "decent" work conditions might be seen as exploitative by another. Similarly, the quality of education isn't just about literacy rates or graduation percentages but involves deeper issues like curriculum content, freedom of thought, and the fostering of critical thinking. The open-ended nature of such terms grants an extensive interpretative leeway. This flexibility, in turn, allows for wildly diverse implementations, not all of which might be genuinely aligned with the true spirit of the SDGs.

- **Potential for Exploitation:** Broad goals are like blank canvases: they can be painted in various hues. While this can be a strength, allowing for cultural and contextual customization, it can also be a significant weakness. Governments or influential entities might co-opt these goals, bending their interpretations to suit their agendas. Under the noble banner of achieving the SDGs, actions might be justified that, under closer examination, serve a narrow interest group or even contravene the broader principles of sustainable development and human rights.

- **Lack of Accountability:** Clear goals lead to clear outcomes. Ambiguous goals, however, muddle the waters. If a goal is framed in vague terms, how does one measure its achievement accurately? This lack of clarity can hinder effective benchmarking and monitoring. After all, if a nation can interpret an SDG in a manner most favorable to its current status or actions, it can easily claim successful progress, even if ground realities tell a different story. This vagueness thus poses a significant challenge in holding nations or organizations truly accountable for their commitments to the SDGs.

In conclusion, while the SDGs are a beacon of hope for many, their very framing can be their Achilles' heel. It is crucial for global stakeholders to acknowledge these pitfalls, engage in clearer delineations of the goals, and establish rigorous monitoring mechanisms. Only then can the true potential of the SDGs be unlocked, ensuring a just, sustainable, and inclusive future for all.

Overreliance on the Private Sector

Concern: The collaboration between the United Nations and the private sector is not just a handshake but a deep intertwining of interests. The question arises: does this partnership serve the global citizenry, or is it a facade that benefits corporate conglomerates more?

In-Depth Examination:

- **Profit vs. Welfare:** Businesses, especially large corporations, operate on a foundational principle: generating profits for shareholders. This isn't necessarily malevolent; it's the nature of capitalism. However, problems arise when these profit-driven motives are embedded within the framework designed to ensure global welfare. In scenarios where corporate interests might clash with those of public welfare, there is a legitimate fear that the scales will tip towards the former. For example, a corporation involved in a clean water project might prioritize regions that promise better returns on investment, leaving impoverished areas, which need it the most, still parched.

- **Regulatory Erosions:** To make the SDG terrain attractive for private entities, governments might dangle the carrot of regulatory relaxations. On paper, these might seem like harmless incentives, but in practice, they could have dire consequences. Relaxing labor regulations might lead to exploitative work conditions, diminishing the promise of 'Decent Work' as per the SDGs. Easing environmental checks could lead to unchecked degradation of natural habitats, contravening the goal of 'Life on Land' or 'Life Below Water'. Such relaxations, while bolstering corporate participation, could be a Trojan horse, ushering in a slew of problems that counteract the benefits of the SDGs.

- **Inequitable Partnerships:** In the global arena, not all nations are equal, at least in terms of bargaining power. Smaller nations, especially those desperate for investments, might find themselves in a David-versus-Goliath scenario when negotiating with multinational corporations. These corporations, armed with vast resources and legal teams, could craft partnerships that disproportionately favor their interests. Such skewed partnerships could see these nations relinquishing more than they gain, be it in terms of natural resources, tax breaks, or even cultural compromises.

In summary, while the private sector's involvement in the SDGs could accelerate progress, it's a double-edged sword. Without careful oversight and a recalibration of priorities, this collaboration might morph into a shadowy dance where corporate interests lead, and global welfare merely follows. The onus, therefore, lies on both the United Nations and national governments to ensure that this partnership remains symbiotic, not parasitic.

Encroachment on Sovereignty:

Concern: At the heart of this intricate web of global goals lies a simple, yet profoundly impactful question: How much should nations compromise on their unique identity, values, and strategies to align with a global vision? There's growing apprehension that in the pursuit of these lofty global goals, individual nations might lose sight of their ground realities and priorities.

In-Depth Examination

Dilution of Cultural Values: Culture is the bedrock on which nations are built. It's a tapestry of traditions, beliefs, and practices passed down through generations. The SDGs, in their universal nature, risk overshadowing these unique cultural narratives. For instance, a goal pushing for gender equality, while noble in its intent, might challenge the deeply rooted cultural beliefs of certain societies. This clash could lead to societal unrest or resistance against the SDGs, labeling them as tools of cultural imperialism.

Economic Pressures: A one-size-fits-all approach might sound efficient, but when it comes to intricate economic ecosystems, it could be calamitous. Each nation has its unique economic strengths, challenges, and strategies, molded by years of experience and adaptation. However, under the shadow of the SDGs, there's a looming threat of countries reshaping their economic policies to fit the global mold. This could jeopardize local industries that can't compete on a global scale, leading to job losses and economic downturns. For example, a push for sustainable agriculture might inadvertently harm small-scale farmers who can't afford sustainable technologies, pushing them further into poverty.

International Peer Pressure: In the global arena, perception matters. No nation wants to be the black sheep, especially when it comes to global initiatives like the SDGs. This desire to conform and be viewed favorably can be a potent tool of coercion. Nations might find themselves toeing the line, not because they believe in the cause, but for fear of diplomatic fallout or international sanctions. Such decisions, driven by external pressures rather than internal convictions, could lead to unrest, as citizens grapple with policies they neither understand nor believe in.

In essence, while the SDGs are painted with the brush of universality, it's crucial to understand that our world is a mosaic of unique nations, each with its own story and journey. Forcing them into a single narrative might not just dilute their essence but could also lead to resistance, rendering the whole exercise counterproductive. As we strive for a better world, it's imperative to ensure that the path we choose respects and celebrates these individual narratives, rather than overshadowing them.

Hidden Agendas?

Concern: Behind the tapestry of 17 interconnected goals, there's a growing suspicion that certain motives remain concealed from the global populace. Could the SDGs be a Trojan Horse, harboring hidden economic and geopolitical strategies of dominant nations and global conglomerates?

In-Depth Examination:

- **Selective Promotions:** The transition to sustainable technologies is no doubt imperative for the planet's survival. However, one can't help but wonder if there's a selective bias in promoting certain technologies over others. For instance, while nuclear energy promises reduced carbon emissions, it comes with its own baggage of nuclear waste and potential disasters. The preference for nuclear over, say, solar or wind energy might not purely be based on its merits. Behind closed doors, intense lobbying by the nuclear industry, combined with the trade dynamics of nations with robust nuclear technology, could be skewing priorities. Such biases could sideline genuinely sustainable options, leaving the world with short-term solutions riddled with long-term repercussions.

- **Economic Interests at Play:** The global stage of economics and trade is a theatre where nations constantly jockey for dominance. The SDGs, with their universal appeal, might just be another stage prop in this play. Let's consider a hypothetical scenario: a goal that emphasizes the digital transformation of economies. On the surface, it promises efficiency and growth. Yet, digging deeper, it might become evident that the primary beneficiaries are tech conglomerates in a few leading nations. As countries rush to digitize, these giants could experience exponential growth, potentially at the cost of local tech industries. Thus, what appears to be a push for global progress might just be a veil for economic colonization by a few.

- **Geopolitical Leverage:** The world map isn't just a depiction of nations; it's a grid of resources, trade routes, and strategic points. Through the SDGs, powerful nations could cunningly position themselves to gain control over these critical aspects. For instance, an SDG emphasizing the importance of secure and sustainable water sources might lead to investments in large-scale water projects. While the stated goal is commendable, this could provide influential nations the leverage to control water sources in strategically vital regions. Such dominance isn't just about the resource; it's a pawn in the intricate game of global politics, trade, and warfare.

In concluding, while the SDGs are presented as a beacon for worldwide unity and development, they require rigorous scrutiny. Like a deceiving mirage, depending on one's perspective and motivations, these goals will reveal hidden agendas, some seemingly harmless and others overtly malevolent. As informed global citizens, we must critically assess and challenge the trajectory set by these goals, understanding that they do not truly serve the broader interests of humanity and our planet but rather cater to a select few.

Chapter 7
Economic and Financial Influence of the UN

<u>Financial Contributions and Implications</u>

Behind the scenes of peacekeeping missions, summits, and global initiatives, the UN's funding mechanism plays a crucial role. Its finances, contributed by member states, raise concerns about the organization's independence, influence, and potential to sway policies to benefit a select few.

Disproportionate Contributions:

Concern: The unbalanced contribution structure, where only a handful of nations bear the majority of the financial responsibilities, potentially bestows these countries with excessive clout in determining the UN's course and focal points.

In-Depth Examination:

- **Financial Might Equals Policy Sway:** Major contributors, such as the United States, China, Germany, and Japan, funnel vast sums into the UN's treasury. Their financial largesse, while essential for the UN's operations, brings up critical concerns. Do these funds come with strings attached? Does this fiscal dominance grant them a bigger say in the crafting and application of UN resolutions, peacekeeping efforts, and global campaigns? If so, the principle of equal representation, which is foundational to the UN's ethos, might be under threat.

- **Unspoken Leverage:** Beyond formal discussions and resolutions, the financial dominance of these nations could manifest in subtler ways. They could employ this financial leverage to expedite initiatives that align with their geopolitical goals or stall actions that challenge their agendas. This might also lead to a scenario where other member nations feel hesitant to voice dissent or contest the direction set by these financial behemoths, given the latter's ability to tighten or loosen the UN's purse strings.

- **Non-State Actors:** Beyond nation-states, the substantial financial inputs of non-state players, exemplified by entities like the Bill & Melinda Gates Foundation, demand attention. Their commendable philanthropic endeavors notwithstanding, their outsized contributions ignite concerns. What role do they play in sculpting worldwide health, educational, and developmental trajectories? Are their financial contributions truly altruistic, or are they strategic investments designed to further specific agendas or industry interests? Such dominant roles by non-state entities could lead to scenarios where the line between philanthropy and influence peddling becomes blurred, thereby undermining the very essence of a multilateral organization like the UN.

Conditional Aid:

Concern: Aid dispensed by UN bodies frequently comes with stipulated conditions, risking the encroachment on the sovereignty of recipient nations, thereby inhibiting their freedom to pursue avenues they deem optimal for their citizens.

In-Depth Examination:

- **Strings Attached:** Aid, especially for nations grappling with poverty, economic instability, or post-conflict reconstruction, can be a lifeline. However, the accompanying terms can sometimes be more than just fiscal accountability measures. Recipient nations might be nudged towards enacting policy reforms, offering trade relaxations, or harmonizing with certain international norms as a quid pro quo for the aid received. While on the surface, these conditions might seem beneficial, there's a deeper concern. Are these stipulations genuinely for the welfare of the recipient, or do they serve to advance the strategic or commercial interests of the donors? Such preconditions can potentially lead nations to adopt decisions that are incongruent with their socio-cultural fabric or economic landscape.

- **Loss of Autonomy:** This conditional form of aid can be construed as an indirect mechanism to erode national sovereignty. The tethering of financial assistance to certain actions subtly shifts the locus of decision-making from the national governments to the corridors of the UN or, more specifically, its dominant financiers. Over time, this could create a dynamic where nations, especially those perennially dependent on aid, become mere proxies, executing a script crafted elsewhere, often in the offices of major donor countries or global financial institutions.

- **Potential for Exploitation:** The very nature of aid suggests a power dynamic – a giver and a receiver. When the giver attaches conditions, it accentuates this power imbalance. There arises a potential, then, for coercion. Nations urgently needing assistance, be it due to natural calamities or economic downturns, might find themselves in a vulnerable position. This desperation can be weaponized, pushing these nations to accede to terms that, under normal circumstances, they'd find unfavorable. This could mean granting access to their natural resources at a pittance, opening their markets to foreign goods without commensurate benefits, or even endorsing geopolitical stances that they might otherwise contest. The guise of aid, in such cases, risks becoming a trojan horse for neo-colonial endeavors.

Financial Dependence

Concern: A multitude of nations are profoundly anchored in the financial assistance provided by the UN. This profound reliance leaves them susceptible to the predispositions and inclinations of the major donor nations, potentially compromising their autonomy and strategic interests.

In-Depth Examination:

- **Vulnerable Positioning:** For many nations, particularly those embroiled in post-conflict scenarios, grappling with economic downturns, or confronting natural calamities, the UN's financial aid isn't just beneficial—it's indispensable. Their heavy reliance on this aid, however, places them on precarious ground. The looming threat of aid withdrawal or reduction can act as a figurative Damocles' sword, dissuading these nations from pursuing policies or stances that might be at odds with the UN's directives, or more pertinently, the interests of its dominant financiers. Such a scenario can subtly compel these nations into a form of diplomatic and policy-oriented subservience, sacrificing their interests for fear of financial reprisals.

- **Swaying Votes and Decisions:** The architecture of the United Nations, particularly in bodies like the General Assembly, hinges on member states casting their votes on a plethora of global issues. However, when financial assistance becomes a tool, or even a weapon, the sacrosanct nature of these votes is jeopardized. Nations heavily reliant on UN's financial aid might find themselves in dilemmas, weighing the pros and cons of voting in line with their genuine stances versus voting in a manner that appeases their financial lifelines. This dynamic threatens the very essence of the UN as a platform for unbiased, sovereign decision-making.

- **Economic Control:** The ripple effects of financial dependence don't stop at policy subservience or vote manipulation. Over prolonged periods, this dependence can pave the way for more insidious forms of control. The UN, or more precisely, its major contributors, could potentially exert a tightening grip over the economic and developmental blueprints of dependent nations. This influence can manifest in myriad ways—dictating trade practices, shaping fiscal policies, or even sculpting developmental agendas. As this control solidifies, there's a burgeoning risk that the unique needs, priorities, and aspirations of local populations might be overshadowed by a one-size-fits-all strategy, designed and endorsed by remote entities with potentially misaligned interests.

The intricate financial dynamics within the UN bring to light potential areas of concern, making it crucial for nations and global observers to remain very vigilant. The vision of a cooperative global body working for the greater good gets muddled when economic influences come into play, compromising the very principles upon which the United Nations was founded.

Economic Sanctions and Their Impacts

Economic sanctions, wielded by the UN, can have profound implications on targeted nations. While they are posed as non-violent means of influencing state behavior, their consequences can be dire and multifaceted, affecting more than just the intended political targets.

Punishing the Innocent

Concern: The blunt instrument of comprehensive economic sanctions, wielded with the intent of destabilizing or reprimanding national regimes, often ends up causing more harm to the ordinary populace than to the intended targets - the governing elite.

In-Depth Examination:

- **Humanitarian Crisis:** When sanctions are imposed, it's not merely a nation's economy that gets affected; it's the very lifeline of its people. Sanctions often block the channels through which essential commodities like food grains, medical supplies, and even basic utilities are imported. Over time, these restrictions can spawn a humanitarian nightmare. Hospitals, already grappling with limited resources, might find themselves bereft of life-saving drugs or equipment. The blockade on food imports can lead to skyrocketing prices in local markets, putting basic nutrition out of reach for many. Children, especially in impoverished households, bear the brunt of this scarcity, with malnutrition rates spiraling upwards. Such scenarios aren't mere hypotheticals; history is replete with instances where sanctions have precipitated dire humanitarian crises.

- **Collateral Damage:** The grim irony of economic sanctions is that while they're often conceptualized as measures to exert pressure on ruling regimes, the real victims tend to be those who have little to no say in national politics. The elderly, who rely on steady medical care and support, face daunting challenges as medical supplies dwindle. Children, particularly in the formative years, face educational disruptions and health challenges. The poor, already perched on the edge of survival, find themselves pushed into further depths of deprivation. All these happen while the political elite, the intended targets, often remain insulated, their lifestyles barely dented by the sanctions.

- **Social Unrest:** The socio-economic tremors caused by sanctions rarely remain confined to just economic metrics. As people grapple with rising prices, dwindling job opportunities, and collapsing essential services, the socio-political fabric of the nation starts to show signs of strain. Unemployment, especially among the youth, can lead to a sense of disillusionment and alienation. This discontent, coupled with the general hardships imposed by the sanctions, can act as a tinderbox. Sporadic protests can escalate into widespread demonstrations, and in extreme cases, the nation might find itself on the brink of civil unrest or even internal conflict. While the ostensible goal of the sanctions might be to bring about political change, they might end up sowing the seeds of long-term instability and strife.

Political Agendas

Concern: The application of economic sanctions, although often presented as a tool for enforcing international norms and ensuring global peace, can sometimes be perceived as an instrument wielded by the powerful to serve their strategic interests, rather than the broader goal of justice.

In-Depth Examination:

- **Selective Targeting:** One only needs to look at the historical tapestry of UN sanctions to observe patterns of selective targeting. While the rationale behind sanctions is typically couched in the language of human rights, nuclear non-proliferation, or global peace, an undercurrent of political motivations often seems to guide these decisions. For instance, certain nations, for comparable infractions, face the brunt of stringent economic blockades, while others, potentially owing to their strategic alliances or economic clout, manage to evade such punitive measures. This inconsistency casts a shadow over the purported impartiality of the UN's sanctions regime, leading many to question whether geopolitical considerations outweigh genuine concerns for global justice.

- **Double Standards:** The perceived double standards become even more glaring when major powers, with their permanent seats and veto powers in the Security Council, appear to sidestep repercussions for their actions. Whether it's interventions in sovereign nations, alleged human rights abuses, or other violations of international norms, these dominant players often remain unscathed, shielded by their diplomatic clout and strategic partnerships. This apparent immunity not only erodes the credibility of the UN's sanctioning mechanism but also fuels allegations of a rigged system, where power dynamics, rather than objective criteria, dictate the course of action.

- **Proxy Conflicts:** The intricate web of global politics frequently gets manifested in the form of proxy conflicts, where major powers, instead of direct confrontations, engage in shadow battles through smaller nations. In these convoluted scenarios, sanctions become more than just punitive measures against a nation's transgressions. They evolve into strategic tools, wielded to weaken an adversary's ally or to exert pressure in a broader geopolitical chess game. The targeted nation, caught in the crossfire of these power plays, often bears the brunt of these economic strictures, not merely for its actions but also because of its position in the larger geopolitical matrix. This adds another layer of complexity to the debate on sanctions, highlighting the intricate interplay of power, politics, and punishment on the global stage.

Economic Manipulation

Concern: Beyond the diplomatic veneer that portrays sanctions as instruments for ensuring global order and adherence to international norms, lies an underbelly of potential economic manipulation. The very nature of sanctions, which affects trade, finance, and economic growth, makes them potent weapons in the arsenal of global economic warfare.

In-Depth Examination:

- **Financial Stranglehold:** The global financial system, anchored by institutions like the SWIFT banking network, World Bank, and IMF, is predominantly influenced by major powers. By denying sanctioned nations access to these platforms, the leading players can essentially isolate them from global commerce and finance. Such isolation can bring a nation's economy to its knees, making them more pliable to the demands or wishes of these dominant entities. This tactic goes beyond just penalizing a country for its purported misdeeds; it's about exerting control and ensuring compliance. In several instances, it's not just about what the sanctioned nation did, but what they might be forced to do under the economic duress of these restrictions.

- **Resource Grab:** History is rife with examples of powers seeking control over territories rich in oil, minerals, and other precious resources. In the modern era, instead of overt colonization, economic tools like sanctions can be wielded to achieve similar ends. By destabilizing an economically vulnerable country through sanctions, dominant powers can create a scenario where the sanctioned nation is left with little choice but to trade its resources at a pittance. This strategy, cloaked in the rhetoric of global peace and security, can serve as a conduit for resource exploitation, where the true objective is not rectification of a global wrong, but a covert economic conquest.

- **Market Dominance:** The global market is a battleground where nations vie for dominance. By sidelining potential competitors through economic sanctions, major powers can ensure that their corporations, products, and services face diminished competition. This can lead to market monopolies or oligopolies where a few players, hailing from the sanctioning nations, dominate the global scene. The consumers, in this scenario, are left with fewer choices, often at higher prices, while the sanctioned nations' industries wither away, unable to compete or access global markets. This is not just about economic dominance; it's about ensuring that the power dynamics, both politically and economically, remain skewed in favor of a select few.

Long-term Consequences

Concern: Economic sanctions, while often portrayed as temporary measures to correct perceived wrongs, can leave a lasting imprint on the targeted nations. These imprints go beyond immediate economic challenges, extending to the very psyche of the nation and its global interactions for generations.

In-Depth Examination:

- **Deepening Mistrust:** The imposition of sanctions, especially when perceived as unjust or disproportionate, can cultivate a deep-seated mistrust in the sanctioned nation towards those that enforced the restrictions. This sentiment can get embedded in the national consciousness, passed down through educational narratives, public discourses, and even popular culture. Over time, such mistrust can solidify into an entrenched skepticism towards international treaties, agreements, or collaborations. This could potentially hinder meaningful dialogue, making conflict resolution or international cooperation far more complex and tedious. It's not just about the immediate pain of the sanctions; it's about the long shadow of distrust they cast on future generations.

- **Alternative Alliances:** When traditional partnerships fray due to sanctions, nations are compelled to seek new friends. This search often leads them to other nations that share similar experiences or views on global power dynamics. These new alliances can challenge the established global order. The sanctioned nations, pooling resources, intelligence, and strategic assets can create blocs that operate counter to the dominant global narrative. Over time, these blocs can evolve into formidable counterweights, challenging the very powers that once imposed sanctions on them. This can lead to a more polarized world, where different factions, driven by past grievances and shared skepticism, work at cross-purposes, diminishing global unity.

- **Economic Scars:** While sanctions are economic tools, their impact isn't merely financial. The economic devastation they cause can cripple industries, erode infrastructures, and deter potential investors long after they are lifted. Rebuilding post-sanctions is not just about reviving the economy; it's about overcoming the stigma associated with being a sanctioned nation. Potential investors, wary of future political instabilities or the potential reimposition of sanctions, might be hesitant to commit capital. Trade partners, too, might be cautious, fearing backlash from dominant powers. This makes the road to economic recovery long and arduous. Beyond the tangible economic setbacks, the intangible impact on national morale, the psyche of the business community, and the aspirations of the youth can be profound, leading to a generation that's skeptical, wary, and, in many ways, disillusioned with the promise of global collaboration.

Sanctions, while painted as instruments of peace, can sometimes be tools of dominance, manipulation, and coercion. The nuanced dynamics around their imposition and their far-reaching impacts underline the need for a more transparent, equitable, and just global order, where economic measures are not wielded as weapons but are genuinely used to foster peace, cooperation, and mutual respect.

In essence, the UN, through its financial mechanisms and economic policies, wields significant power over the global economic landscape. While on the surface, these tools are touted as means to ensure global stability and prosperity, a closer examination reveals potential avenues for control, manipulation, and coercion. It prompts the question: Is the UN a benign overseer of global peace and cooperation, or does it operate as a shadowy puppeteer, pulling the strings of global finance and economy to serve a grander, perhaps more sinister, design?

Chapter 8
Concerns Over National Sovereignty

Cases of Potential Compromise

The concept of national sovereignty – the idea that a state should have exclusive authority over its territory and domestic affairs – stands at a crossroads in the age of globalization. The UN, as the foremost international organization, often finds itself embroiled in debates concerning its role in potentially undermining this sovereignty.

Interventionist Policies

Concern: The mandate of the UN, ostensibly created to foster peace and cooperation among nations, has often been called into question due to its peacekeeping interventions. While the idea of maintaining global peace is universally accepted as noble, the means and methods employed by the UN have been points of contention.

In-Depth Examination:

- **Veiled Agendas:** When the UN dispatches peacekeeping forces, the global community expects a neutral intervention with the sole aim of restoring peace. However, critics opine that these missions can be tainted with clandestine objectives. Taking the Libya case as an example, what was publicized as a mission of mercy to safeguard innocent lives took a different trajectory, leading to the toppling of a regime. This sudden shift in objectives fueled speculations of underlying geopolitical strategies at play. The aftermath? Libya, a once prosperous nation, became a hotbed of civil unrest, militia rule, and chaos. One might question whether the UN's intervention, influenced by powerful nations, inadvertently paved the way for such a breakdown.

- **Selective Interventions:** The UN's decision-making process on where to deploy peacekeepers is under constant scrutiny. Observers point out glaring inconsistencies in the organization's approach. There are places with rampant human rights violations and escalating conflicts that remain untouched by the UN's peacekeeping endeavors. Why this disparity? Skeptics believe that this selectivity is not random. They argue that global superpowers, wielding significant influence in UN's administrative corridors, shape these decisions to align with their strategic objectives. This perspective posits that the sanctity of the UN's neutral stance is, at times, sacrificed at the altar of power politics.

- **Long-term Occupation:** Peacekeeping, by definition, is expected to be a temporary measure — a bridge to stability until the host nation can reclaim control. But in some scenarios, these missions morph into long-term engagements, with UN troops staying on foreign soils for years, even decades. Critics view such prolonged presences as reminiscent of colonial occupations. In these prolonged missions, the UN's role often expands beyond maintaining peace. They become key players in local governance, resource allocation, and socio-economic developments. Over time, the lines blur between a peacekeeping mission and a governance structure, leading to accusations that the UN, under the guise of peacekeeping, assumes the role of a pseudo-governing entity, thereby undermining the very essence of national sovereignty.

Imposed Mandates

Concern: The United Nations, an institution supposedly founded on the principles of collective decision-making and equality among nations, has mechanisms that, in practice, seem to subvert these ideals. The dynamics within its core bodies, particularly the Security Council, raise eyebrows over the genuine preservation of national interests.

In-Depth Examination:

- **Veto Power:** Central to the debate on the fairness of the UN's decision-making process is the veto power enjoyed by the five permanent members of the Security Council. Historically, this mechanism was intended to prevent unilateral decisions and ensure cooperative solutions. However, critics argue that this has turned into a tool for power politics. With the ability to block any resolution, these five nations can steer global policies according to their whims and strategic interests. As a result, crucial resolutions, which might have been beneficial for the global community, can be stonewalled if they don't align with the interests of any of these five nations. This setup raises an essential question: Is the global order being held hostage to the interests of a privileged few?

- **Enforced Compliance:** The UN's resolutions, especially those emanating from the Security Council, come with a weight of global legitimacy. However, the enforcement of these resolutions can be skewed. Nations that dare to challenge or sidestep these mandates can be subjected to punitive measures, ranging from economic sanctions to military interventions. While the UN might project these as measures to uphold international law, detractors see them as tools to strong-arm nations into submission. The implications are profound. Sovereign countries, in trying to protect their global standing and economic interests, might be compelled to act against their internal consensus or national strategies, leading to internal discontent and political upheaval.

- **Sidelining Voices:** The UN charter underscores the principle of sovereign equality, implying that all member nations, big or small, have an equal voice. However, the ground realities paint a different picture. Smaller nations, especially those from the Global South or those lacking the patronage of global superpowers, often find their voices drowned in the cacophony of power politics. Their interests, priorities, and concerns can be easily brushed aside in the face of dominant narratives. This dynamic not only contradicts the UN's foundational principles but also breeds disillusionment among member states. Feeling unheard and marginalized, these nations might question the very efficacy and relevance of the institution, potentially seeking alternative avenues to voice their concerns and safeguard their interests.

Trade and Economic Policies

Concern: Economic sovereignty is foundational for a nation's path to development and self-determination. However, the UN, along with its associated agencies, can exert influences that challenge a nation's ability to determine its economic fate. Such interventions can sometimes be more about serving global or powerful interests than they are about the well-being of the citizens of the affected countries.

In-Depth Examination:

- **Structural Adjustments:** The role of institutions like the International Monetary Fund (IMF) and the World Bank in shaping the economic trajectories of nations cannot be overstated. Over the decades, their structural adjustment programs (SAPs) have come under intense scrutiny. These programs, ostensibly designed to stabilize faltering economies, demand significant economic restructuring in return for financial assistance. However, the conditions they impose often lean heavily towards neoliberal economic policies. These can involve austerity measures, liberalization, privatization, and deregulation. The purported rationale is that these changes spur economic growth. In reality, however, these programs can erode public services, increase inequality, and place the burden of economic recovery on the most vulnerable segments of society. What's even more concerning is the perceived lack of agency among recipient nations, as these changes aren't so much choices as they are mandates.

- **Economic Coercion:** In a globalized world, economic relations are deeply intertwined, and this interdependence can be both a boon and a tool for manipulation. The UN-backed global economic framework, with its intricate web of trade relations, financial flows, and investment networks, provides ample avenues for exerting pressure. Nations that diverge from accepted global norms, challenge powerful entities, or stand up for their sovereign rights might find themselves economically isolated. This can manifest in various ways: from being shut out of global trade forums, facing targeted sanctions, losing preferential trade status, or witnessing sudden flight of foreign investments. Such economic arm-twisting can cripple economies, leading to public distress and potentially forcing governments to capitulate to external pressures against the wishes and well-being of their citizens.

- **Cultural Insensitivity:** Economic policies aren't just about numbers; they are deeply intertwined with the social and cultural fabric of nations. A top-down, one-size-fits-all approach, often propagated by global bodies, can be fundamentally flawed. It can overlook ground realities, indigenous knowledge, and local nuances. For instance, promoting cash crops over traditional farming might boost exports in the short term but can lead to long-term environmental degradation, loss of biodiversity, and food insecurity. Pushing for rapid industrialization without understanding local dynamics can lead to land grabs, displacement of communities, and loss of traditional livelihoods. Such policies, while looking good on paper, can have devastating consequences on the ground, leading to local upheavals, deep-seated resentments, and a sense of cultural erosion.

The tension between the ideals of international cooperation and national sovereignty is palpable. As the UN wields considerable power and influence, it becomes crucial to ensure that this power is exercised judiciously, respecting the sanctity of each nation's unique identity, aspirations, and sovereignty.

Balance between Global Governance and National Autonomy

The United Nations, while embodying the aspiration of global peace and cooperation, has, over time, faced criticism regarding its interference in the sovereignty of member nations. The line between global governance and national autonomy is a blurry one, and the UN's actions sometimes seem to oscillate between the two, leading to contentious debates.

Global Standards vs. Local Needs

Depth of Diversity: Our planet is rich in its array of cultures, each with its own intricacies and nuances. Societies, from the vast expanse of Africa to the sprawling archipelagos of Southeast Asia, have developed unique ways of life, governance, and social structures over millennia. Each nation's narrative is deeply interwoven with its past, its struggles, triumphs, invasions, revolutions, and more. Every piece of this historical tapestry has led to the present-day identity of a nation. Within this context, the United Nations, in its quest for global homogenization, may inadvertently undermine the rich tapestry of global diversity. The risk is that global standards, while well-intentioned, may not always appreciate or incorporate the deep-rooted traditions and values that form the core of a nation's identity.

Examples of Dissonance: The pursuit of global standards, especially in areas like development, has frequently led to tensions. Developed nations, having already achieved a certain level of industrialization and prosperity, often champion sustainable practices. Their infrastructures, economies, and societal expectations are built around these practices. However, for many developing nations, the immediate concerns revolve around basic survival, job creation, and poverty alleviation. They're in the phase of industrial evolution that developed nations passed through decades or even centuries ago. Asking a nation, where a significant portion of the population lacks basic amenities like clean water or electricity, to prioritize the same environmental standards as a developed country isn't just impractical, it's tone-deaf. It disregards the immediate necessities of nations and the paths they need to traverse for their progress.

Economic Implications: The economic trajectory of a nation is closely tied to its developmental phase. Emerging economies are often in the throes of rapid industrialization, seeking to establish themselves in the global marketplace. However, global standards, especially those championed by the UN and its allied bodies, can sometimes act as barriers. For instance, a country in Africa, rich in minerals, might be on the cusp of establishing a mining industry. But stringent global environmental norms might stymie its progress. Similarly, global trade policies could be skewed, favoring established markets and making it challenging for newcomers to gain a foothold. This is not to undermine the importance of environmental conservation or fair trade, but it underscores the importance of understanding the context. For a nation aiming to feed its hungry, provide jobs to its youth, and ensure a better life for its citizens, these global restrictions can feel like a straitjacket, stifling their growth and aspirations.

In sum, while the intention behind global governance is laudable, its implementation often lacks nuance. The delicate balance between what the world deems right and what a nation deems necessary is a tightrope walk. The United Nations, in its endeavors, must be wary of the fine line between guidance and imposition, between global standards and local needs.

Diplomatic Pressures

Power Dynamics: At the heart of the United Nations lies a foundational paradox. While it was established with the noble objective of representing all nations and their voices, the actual power structure within its primary decision-making body, the Security Council, seems to defy this egalitarian principle. The presence of five permanent members—United States, Russia, China, United Kingdom, and France— with the authority to veto any substantive resolution, has often led to a monopolistic dynamic. This structure inherently prioritizes the interests of these nations over the majority. Over the years, many countries, especially those from the developing world, have expressed concerns about this glaring imbalance of power. They argue that their sovereign rights and voices are suppressed under the weight of the 'Big Five'. This sentiment can create a perception that the UN, instead of being a beacon of global democracy, leans towards an oligarchic setup.

Proxy Battles: History has shown that the halls of the United Nations can sometimes resemble a grand theater, where powerful nations play out their geopolitical strategies. The Cold War era was a testament to this, where the U.S. and the Soviet Union, without firing a single bullet at each other, engaged in intense diplomatic warfare, rallying allies and using the UN as a battleground for ideological supremacy. But the ramifications of these proxy battles extend beyond just these superpowers. Smaller nations, often without any stake in these larger conflicts, find themselves caught in the crossfire. They might be pressured, through means both overt and covert, to take sides. This can range from economic incentives to more nefarious methods like threats of sanctions or military intervention. The result? Many of these nations, instead of using the UN as a platform to further their national interests, find themselves navigating a minefield of global power plays. Their diplomatic stances might be less about their sovereign choices and more about the pressures exerted upon them.

In essence, while the United Nations stands as a symbol of global cooperation, the underlying dynamics paint a more complex picture. The power imbalances and the high-stakes diplomatic games can sometimes overshadow the very principles the institution was built upon. For a smaller nation, navigating this intricate web of global diplomacy can be challenging, often forcing them into positions that might not necessarily align with their national ethos or aspirations. The question then arises—does the current structure of the UN truly serve the purpose of collective global good, or does it merely amplify the agendas of the powerful few?

Loss of Cultural Identity

The Homogenization Concern: The tapestry of our world is woven with an intricate blend of languages, traditions, rituals, and histories that define the identity of nations and peoples. These cultural treasures have been cultivated over millennia, representing the shared memories and experiences of entire communities. With the ever-growing wave of globalization, driven in part by the UN's promotion of universal values and standards, there emerges a real threat of cultural assimilation. The more countries are encouraged—or sometimes pressured—to conform to a single global norm, the more these individual threads risk being overshadowed. One can draw parallels to a vast forest where unique species are gradually replaced by a single dominant tree, leading to a loss of ecological richness. Similarly, as nations feel the need to fit into a global mold, their cultural identities might get compromised, leading to a more monolithic and less diverse global society.

Implication on Indigenous Populations: At the intersection of the global and the local lie the indigenous communities. These communities, with their age-old traditions, have lived in harmony with nature and have safeguarded the wisdom of their ancestors. However, the story of modern civilization hasn't been as kind to them. Many have been dislocated, their rights trampled upon, and their voices muted. The UN's drive for establishing global standards, if not carefully curated, can inadvertently exacerbate these challenges. For instance, global conservation efforts might prioritize preserving certain ecosystems but might overlook the rights of indigenous communities who inhabit them. While the intention is noble, the road to such global good can sometimes be paved with local injustices. The vital knowledge and practices that these communities bring to the global table risk being lost in the cacophony of universal values.

Cultural Diplomacy: The art of diplomacy extends beyond just politics and economics—it encapsulates the broader engagement of cultures. When the United Nations and its allied organizations push aggressively for a set of global norms, without taking into account the cultural sensitivities of individual nations, they risk not only sidelining those nations but also sowing seeds of resentment. Such a top-down approach can be perceived as cultural imperialism by some nations, leading them to further entrench themselves in their cultural cocoons. Instead of the UN being a bridge between cultures, fostering mutual respect and understanding, it can inadvertently become a bulldozer, paving over the rich diversity of global cultures. In the long run, such a strategy is counterproductive, as it breeds mistrust and reduces the willingness of nations to cooperate on other pressing global issues.

In conclusion, while the pursuit of global norms and values is commendable, it's imperative for organizations like the United Nations to tread cautiously. The world's cultural diversity is its strength, and any endeavor that risks diminishing this richness needs careful introspection. It's a delicate balance between global unity and local identity, one that requires a nuanced and respectful approach.

Question of Accountability

Structural Limitations: The United Nations, heralded as the beacon of global cooperation, finds itself enmeshed in an intricate web of bureaucracy and politics. Its structure, characterized by assemblies, councils, and commissions, is a double-edged sword. On one hand, it's designed to represent the voice of 193 member states, while on the other, it lends itself to manipulation by a few influential players. This is particularly evident in the Security Council, where the five permanent members wield the power of the veto, effectively controlling the decisions of the council. This concentration of power can lead to situations where decisions, or the lack thereof, are driven not by the collective good of the global community, but by the strategic interests of a select few. This opacity in decision-making, coupled with a lack of transparency, makes it an arduous task to pinpoint responsibility and, subsequently, hold the institution accountable for its actions or inactions.

Legal Implications: Venturing into the labyrinth of international law, one quickly discerns that it's not as black and white as domestic legal systems. The UN, with its diplomatic immunity and status as an intergovernmental organization, occupies a privileged position. It's shielded, to a great extent, from legal repercussions that might stem from its actions. This raises a contentious question: if a decision or intervention by the UN leads to adverse outcomes for a country—be it economic hardships, socio-political turmoil, or even loss of life—does that nation have any legal recourse against the global body? The prevailing complexities and intricacies of international law make it an area rife with ambiguities. Thus, while nations may cry foul, seeking justice in a legal sense remains an uphill battle.

The Role of the Secretary-General: At the helm of the UN stands the Secretary-General, often perceived as the embodiment of the ideals and objectives of the organization. However, the reality is more nuanced. Contrary to popular belief, the Secretary-General doesn't wield absolute power; rather, the role is circumscribed by the mandate of mediation, coordination, and administration. Decisions, especially those with far-reaching implications, are often the collective outcome of various organs within the UN. This decentralization of authority, while democratically commendable, poses a conundrum. When actions of the UN infringe upon a nation's sovereignty or lead to undesirable outcomes, pinpointing accountability becomes a quagmire. Is it the Secretary-General, a specific council, a commission, or the entire conglomerate of member states that should be held responsible? This dispersion of power, rather than clarifying lines of responsibility, further muddies the waters of accountability.

In essence, the quest for accountability within the behemoth that is the United Nations is akin to navigating a maze with constantly shifting walls. While the organization stands as a symbol of global unity and cooperation, its structural and legal intricacies make it a formidable challenge for nations to hold it answerable, especially when their sovereignty feels threatened.

The United Nations, in its quest to foster global cooperation, faces the mammoth task of balancing diverse national interests. While its goals might have been noble, the path is fraught with challenges. Nations, in their interaction with the UN, must remain very vigilant, ensuring that their governments, sovereignty, and unique identity, aren't compromised in the name of global governance.

Global Governance vs. Global Dominance: The UN's Veiled Intentions

At the crossroads of geopolitics and global aspirations stand the concepts of Global Governance and Global Dominance. These two terms, while uttered in the same breath, herald contrasting futures for the global community. And the institution at the heart of these discussions is the

United Nations, a behemoth that purportedly stands as the guardian of global cooperation. Yet, a critical examination of its trajectory raises poignant questions about its genuine intentions.

Global Governance signifies an era where nations no longer function as isolated entities, walled by their borders. Instead, they engage in a dance of diplomacy, mutual respect, and collective decision-making. This approach celebrates the tapestry of diverse cultures, governance models, and aspirations that make up the global community. The gravitas of Global Governance lies in its promise of harmonizing the collective might of nations to address the formidable challenges that no country can combat alone. Whether it's the devastating sweep of pandemics, the existential dread of climate change, or the intricacies of global trade dynamics, Global Governance offers a framework for shared responsibility and action.

Global Dominance, in stark contrast, conjures a dystopian vision. It heralds a world order steeped in power dynamics, where decisions are not the culmination of collective wisdom but are dictated by a dominant entity or a consortium of powerful actors. In this paradigm, the notion of sovereignty becomes fragile, as nations find their choices, policies, and futures swayed, or even dictated, by a centralized authority. The peril of this approach is that it risks silencing the diverse voices of smaller or less influential nations, instead of championing an overarching narrative that may not cater to the unique needs and aspirations of all.

Within the marbled halls of the United Nations, amidst the fluttering flags representing 193 member states, there exists a duality. On the surface, the UN heralds itself as the paragon of Global Governance. It parades a narrative of unity, emphasizing global collaboration to surmount challenges and build a brighter future for all. Yet, skeptics and critics, armed with a discerning lens, argue that there's more than meets the eye.

Whispers of the UN's overreach, its interventions in domestic affairs of sovereign nations under the guise of "humanitarian efforts" or "global standards," have been persistent. The institution's influence in sculpting global economic policies, often favoring powerful nations, multi-nationals, or global elites, has not gone unnoticed. Additionally, the push for uniform global policies, while ostensibly framed as attempts at creating a cohesive global framework, sidelines the unique needs and circumstances of individual nations most of the times.

So, while the United Nations may drape itself in the garb of Global Governance, it's imperative for nations and global citizens alike to be very discerning. Vigilance is essential to ensure that we don't let the promise of cooperative global leadership morph into a subtle, yet inexorable, slide towards Global Dominance that it is clearly heading to. For in that lies the risk of a world order that, instead of celebrating diversity and mutual respect, enforces uniformity and centralization, at the cost of the unique identities, sovereignties of nations, and most importantly, our freedoms.

Chapter 9
The Underbelly of UN-Backed Institutions: Power, Corruption, and Elitism

While the United Nations (UN) and its associated agencies have been key in promoting international cooperation, peace, and development, there are numerous accusations and concerns regarding their operations, especially around abuse of power, corruption, bias, and favoring elites. In this chapter, we delve into these issues, unpacking the controversies and criticisms associated with these agencies.

World Health Organization (WHO)

The WHO, a specialized agency of the United Nations responsible for international public health, was established in 1948. It was tasked with the commendable goal of ensuring better health outcomes for people across the globe. However, its voyage has not been free from turbulence.

Critique: Over the years, there have been numerous allegations suggesting that the WHO is swayed by the tentacles of powerful pharmaceutical giants. These suspicions posit that the organization might manipulate or even distort public health guidelines, placing the interests of these companies over the well-being of global citizens. Such potential entwinement with profit-driven entities casts shadows over its purportedly noble objectives. Additionally, the WHO's competence was thrust into the limelight during the initial stages of the COVID-19 pandemic. Many believe that the organization's delayed response and seemingly ambiguous guidelines exacerbated the crisis, leading to global repercussions.

UNESCO (The United Nations Educational, Scientific and Cultural Organization)

UNESCO, founded in 1945, promotes international collaboration in the domains of education, science, culture, and communication. Its most recognizable endeavor is perhaps the designation of World Heritage Sites, locales of immense natural or cultural significance.

Critique: Despite its noble aspirations, UNESCO's activities have not been devoid of controversies. Critics argue that the process of designating World Heritage Sites is marred by political bias. There are instances where certain locations, despite their undeniable value, are overlooked, while others are promoted due to underlying geopolitical currents or lobbying. Such perceived partiality dilutes the sanctity of the designation and undermines the institution's credibility.

UNICEF (The United Nations Children's Fund)

Established in 1946, UNICEF's mission is to provide emergency food and healthcare to children in countries that had been devastated by World War II. Over time, it evolved to address long-term developmental needs of children and women in developing countries.

Critique: As with any large-scale global organization, UNICEF has faced its share of criticisms. Some of the most damning concern the organization's financial workings. Allegations of financial mismanagement, combined with perceived bureaucratic lethargy, have at times overshadowed its many successes. Additionally, there's growing concern about the extent to which large corporate donors, such as The Bill & Melinda Gates Foundation, influence UNICEF's policies and initiatives. Critics question whether such influential backers could steer the organization's agenda, potentially sidelining or diluting initiatives that may not align with these donors' perspectives or interests.

UNDP (United Nations Development Programme)

The UNDP is the United Nations' global development network, advocating for change and connecting countries to knowledge, experience, and resources to help people build a better life. Since its inception in 1965, the UNDP has made strides in its mission to eradicate poverty, reduce inequalities, and build resilience to crises.

Critique: However, the institution has not been without its share of criticism. Detractors frequently question the efficacy of its development programs. Allegations suggest that a considerable chunk of funds don't reach the intended beneficiaries, either due to bureaucratic red tape or outright misuse. Instead of making a direct impact on the ground, vast sums are reportedly lost to administrative overheads or even corruption. This paints a picture of an institution where the noble intent gets bogged down by operational inefficiencies and potential malfeasance.

UNHCR (United Nations High Commissioner for Refugees)

Founded in 1950, the UNHCR's primary purpose is to safeguard the rights and well-being of refugees. Tasked with ensuring that everyone can exercise the right to seek asylum and find refuge in another state, the organization has been at the forefront of numerous humanitarian efforts globally.

Critique: But the luster of its commendable mission is, at times, tarnished by allegations of mismanagement. Refugee camps, which fall under the purview of the UNHCR, have come under scrutiny for sub-par living conditions. Reports of unsanitary environments, lack of adequate food and medical care, and, most disturbingly, insecurity where inhabitants, especially women and children, face threats, are commonplace. Such conditions raise questions about the agency's capability, or perhaps willingness, to uphold its mandate effectively.

UNEP (United Nations Environment Programme)

Established in 1972 following the United Nations Conference on the Human Environment, the UNEP serves as the voice for the environment within the United Nations system. Its mission is to provide leadership and encourage partnerships in caring for the environment.

Critique: Despite its high objectives, UNEP has had its fair share of critics. Many feel that the organization is more preoccupied with the spectacle rather than substance. Accusations suggest a propensity for high-profile global conferences, often seen as talking shops that yield little actionable outcomes. Critics argue that while UNEP remains active in churning out what some label as "climate propaganda," it is lacking in meaningful on-ground action. The perceived gap between its grand pronouncements and tangible outcomes in environmental conservation further fuels skepticism.

FAO (Food and Agriculture Organization of the United Nations)

The FAO is a specialized agency of the United Nations that leads international efforts to defeat hunger and improve nutrition and food security. Its tasks include offering support to countries in their agricultural and nutritional endeavors and ensuring that people have regular access to high-quality food to lead active, healthy lives.

Critique: Notwithstanding its aspirational goals, FAO has faced its own set of criticisms. A significant contention surrounds its promotion of specific agricultural practices. Skeptics suggest that such endorsements appear to align more with the interests of multinational agribusinesses rather than the sustenance and growth of small farmers. This purported alignment seemingly compromises the interests of local agriculture, potentially pushing them towards practices unsuitable to their specific contexts. Furthermore, FAO's involvement in promoting reduced fertilizer use has been construed by some as a bid to push the broader climate change agenda of the UN, without adequately considering the nuanced requirements of diverse agricultural ecosystems.

ILO (International Labour Organization)

The ILO brings together governments, employers, and workers to set labor standards, develop policies, and devise programs promoting decent work for all women and men. Its core mandate is to promote rights at work, encourage decent employment opportunities, and enhance social protection.

Critique: While the ILO's mission is undeniably critical, its execution has not been without detractors. Concerns have arisen suggesting that the organization, on occasions, seems to prioritize the interests of big businesses at the expense of workers, especially in developing countries. These apprehensions highlight potential inconsistencies in ILO's policy endorsements and on-ground realities, suggesting that the rights of workers in vulnerable economies might be compromised in favor of business interests.

WFP (World Food Programme)

The World Food Programme is the food assistance branch of the United Nations. It is the world's largest humanitarian organization focused on hunger and food security, working towards ensuring that everyone, especially children, has access to the food they need.

Critique: For all its monumental efforts, WFP has not been spared scrutiny. Critics frequently highlight alleged inefficiencies in its food distribution processes. Claims abound of food aid either being significantly delayed, misrouted, or, in some unfortunate instances, not reaching the intended recipients at all. Such inefficiencies, whether systemic or isolated, put vulnerable populations at further risk, undermining the very ethos of the organization.

World Bank

The World Bank, a financial institution that offers financial and technical assistance to developing countries, aims to reduce poverty and support development. It provides loans, grants, and expert advice to aid countries in building infrastructure, health, and education systems, and address various other development issues.

Critique: Despite its stated objectives of poverty alleviation, the World Bank has faced significant backlash. Critics argue that it often serves as a tool for Western economic dominance, pushing developing nations into the clutches of debt. By advocating neoliberal policies, the Bank has been accused of inadvertently, or even purposefully, promoting increased inequality, thereby destabilizing societies, and fostering social unrest. The resultant economic imbalances often make these countries more dependent on external aid, thus exacerbating the cycle of debt and dependence.

WTO (World Trade Organization)

The World Trade Organization regulates international trade. Through its main function of producing trade agreements, the WTO aims to ensure that trade flows smoothly, predictably, and as freely as possible between its member nations.

Critique: At the heart of the criticisms levied against the WTO lies the contention that it perpetuates a skewed system. Critics opine that the WTO's trade rules often play into the hands of developed nations and powerful multinational corporations, thus sidelining the interests and potential growth of developing countries. Such a lopsided power dynamic, not only restricts developing countries' economic growth but also undermines the global ethos of fair trade.

IMF (International Monetary Fund)

An international organization created to foster global monetary cooperation and financial stability, the IMF offers monetary support and expert advice to its member countries. It aims to facilitate balanced growth of international trade and provide resources to assist member countries in need of financial help.

Critique: The IMF, much like its counterpart the World Bank, has not been immune to allegations of perpetuating economic hardships in the countries it pledges to assist. Critics have highlighted the often stringent conditions attached to its loans, demanding structural adjustments that may not always align with the recipient nation's socio-economic fabric. These conditions, not only exacerbate economic vulnerabilities but also impinge upon national sovereignty. References have been made to demands that range from controlling fiscal policies to acquiring rights to precious resources, like minerals, thereby potentially jeopardizing the recipient country's long-term prospects.

WMO (World Meteorological Organization)

The World Meteorological Organization is a specialized agency of the United Nations that is responsible for promoting international cooperation in meteorology, climatology, operational hydrology, and related geophysical sciences.

Critique: Despite its seemingly uncontroversial mandate, the WMO has not escaped criticism. Detractors question its effectiveness in truly fostering international cooperation on weather-related matters. The more vociferous of these critics argue that the WMO perpetuates certain narratives on climate change that may not always be rooted in comprehensive scientific data. These so-called "false claims" are believed by some to exert undue influence on global policies, potentially causing nations to invest in mitigation strategies that might not offer the most optimal outcomes.

IAEA (International Atomic Energy Agency)

Established as the world's center for cooperation in the nuclear field, the IAEA seeks to promote the safe, secure, and peaceful use of nuclear energy, assisting its member states in planning for and using nuclear science and technology for various peaceful means.

Critique: The IAEA's reputation has been marred by accusations of harboring a Western bias. Critics point to what they perceive as an unequal scrutiny of nuclear programs across countries. Some nations are subjected to rigorous inspections and sanctions, while others seemingly escape the same degree of oversight. Moreover, while nuclear power is recognized by many experts as a cleaner alternative to fossil fuels in terms of carbon emissions, the IAEA's perceived bias has led to questions about its genuine commitment to promoting its peaceful and environment-friendly use.

UNIDO (United Nations Industrial Development Organization)

UNIDO is a specialized agency that aims to promote and accelerate inclusive and sustainable industrial development in developing countries and economies in transition.

Critique: UNIDO's role in supporting industrialization in developing nations has come under fire. Critics argue that rather than truly bolstering local industries, the organization's initiatives often end up benefiting multinational corporations disproportionately. Such preferential treatment, they contend, undermines local businesses, leading to a loss of local jobs and dilution of indigenous cultures. Furthermore, this dynamic allegedly funnels wealth into the hands of these global corporations, exacerbating economic disparities and potentially hindering genuine, grassroots-level development.

In Conclusion

The mounting critiques against these institutions are not just an indication of operational gaps but also hint at deeper structural and ideological issues. As these narratives gain momentum, the global community must confront these concerns head-on, reassessing the roles and methodologies of such influential organizations. Whether these critiques emerge from grounded realities or conspiracy theories, they serve as a reminder of the importance of continual scrutiny and the quest for a more equitable global order.

Chapter 10
UN's Quest for Global Dominance

Evidence of Intent:

Evidence abounds in various corners of discourse that the United Nations, under the guise of peacekeeping and global development, might be fostering a deeper intent: establishing dominance over the world's nations and centralizing global power. Here's a deeper exploration into the evidence cited:

Documented Declarations:

One can't overlook certain moments where the veil seems to have been lifted, albeit briefly, revealing a possible underlying intent of the UN. There have been documents and statements from UN officials that have overtly or covertly mentioned the aspiration for a more centralized global governance. Such documents are pivotal for they show the UN's intent in black and white. Critics argue that these are not just coincidental mentions but rather give insight into the organization's longer-term vision of a world where power dynamics are drastically shifted, with the UN at the helm.

Unification of Laws:

Uniformity can sometimes be synonymous with control. The UN's fervent push for standardized laws across nations—particularly in domains like human rights, environment, and trade—seems like a clear effort to create a harmonized global narrative. While on the surface, it projects the intent of creating a world bound by similar values and rights, critics argue that this is a systematic strategy to homogenize the global order. By ensuring that nations abide by similar legal frameworks, the UN ensures a certain level of control over nation-specific agendas.

International Courts:

The very existence of bodies such as the International Criminal Court (ICC) raises eyebrows for some. Why? Because it embodies the concept of a judiciary that isn't bound by national borders. While the ICC is tasked with prosecuting individuals for international crimes, its power to override national jurisdictions is seen by critics as a demonstration of the UN's aspiration to centralize legal authority. The apprehension is that this is just the beginning, and with time, the power and scope of such international courts might only expand, diminishing the legal sovereignty of individual nations.

Agenda 21 and Agenda 2030:

On the face of it, these agendas, emphasizing global sustainability, seem noble and necessary. The planet needs collective action to counter challenges like "climate change", environmental degradation, and socioeconomic disparities. However, the devil, as they say, is in the details. Critics argue that embedded within these agendas is a strategic blueprint for the UN's centralized control over resources, economies, and policies. The recommendation for streamlined urban development, sustainable resource management, and global partnerships, while crucial, could also be mechanisms for the UN to dictate terms and control the course of global development.

While it's essential to approach these critiques with a balanced perspective, one can't dismiss them as mere conspiracy theories. They raise fundamental questions about power, sovereignty, and the future of nations in a rapidly globalizing world. As the UN continues its quest for global betterment, its actions, decisions, and documents will be under increased scrutiny from those who fear a shift towards global dominance.

<u>Highlights of the UN Achieving Global Dominance:</u>

The implications of the UN's perceived intent of gaining global dominance are vast and varied. Two major aspects of such a vision, centralized control, and its supposed advantages and negatives, warrant a more in-depth exploration.

Centralized Control:

Centralized control speaks to the notion of consolidating global governance under one major umbrella entity, streamlining the bureaucratic processes and aiming to create a world that operates in a more harmonized manner. However, as with all facets of governance, there are both potential benefits and pitfalls.

- **Supposed Advantage:** The chief advantage often touted for centralized control is efficiency. By bringing governance under a single authority, the process of decision-making becomes streamlined, and the implementation of international policies becomes more uniform. There's no inter-country squabbling, no waiting for individual nations to ratify treaties, and a consistent approach to global issues. This could mean that global crises, like pandemics or environmental challenges, are addressed with a swiftness and unity previously unseen. But here lies the question – at what cost does this efficiency come?

- **Negative Side:** The darker side of centralized control emerges when one digs deeper into what this means for individual freedoms and the autonomy of regions and nations. Regional differences, be it in terms of culture, economics, or social values, are the heartbeats of our diverse world. By trying to fit diverse regions into a one-size-fits-all mold, we risk losing the essence of that diversity.

Such a single governing entity, while efficient, might lack the intricate understanding needed to address the nuanced needs of different regions. For example, an agricultural policy that works wonders for European countries might wreak havoc when enforced in African regions. This lack of regional consideration could lead to regulations that ignore or even harm individual territories' specific needs and preferences.

Moreover, when power is consolidated, there's an inherent risk of that power being misused or concentrated in the hands of a few elite. With the absence of checks and balances that come with multiple governing bodies, there's potential for abuse.

Lastly, the very essence of democracy is based on representation. In a centralized model, can every nation, especially smaller ones, truly feel they have a voice? Or would they be drowned out by the larger players? Such feelings of marginalization could lead to widespread discontent, potentially sparking protests or even uprisings.

In essence, while the allure of centralized control under the UN promises a vision of efficiency and unified direction, it also carries significant risks. Risks that could change the very fabric of global society, potentially undermining the diverse cultures, traditions, and values that make our world so unique.

Resource Allocation:

The notion of a global entity like the U.N. having complete control over the world's resources is a profound one, laden with implications for every nation, community, and individual. Centralizing resource allocation could dramatically shift the world's economic and power dynamics.

- **Supposed Advantage:** Resource allocation, in its essence, pertains to the distribution of wealth, commodities, and access to essential elements like food, water, energy, and infrastructure. Under the centralized vision of the U.N., the distribution of these resources would be controlled through a singular lens, presumably based on needs and equitable principles. This could potentially lead to a world where resources are no longer hoarded or monopolized by a few powerful nations or entities. Developing nations, historically exploited and sidelined, might see an uptick in resources, leading to improved living conditions, infrastructure, and economic growth.

The argument here is that a singular entity, unhindered by national biases or political considerations, could distribute resources more fairly, aiming for global betterment. Ideally, resources could be redirected swiftly to regions in crisis, like during famines, droughts, or after natural disasters, without bureaucratic delays or geopolitical hesitations.

- **Negative Side:** But as with all visions of consolidated power, there's a much darker underbelly to this scenario. With absolute control comes the temptation of absolute corruption. The adage "Power corrupts, and absolute power corrupts absolutely" rings especially true here.

In a world where the U.N. controls all resources, what mechanisms would be in place to check and balance this power? If a particular nation or region were to question the U.N.'s decisions or challenge its authority, they could potentially find themselves at the mercy of the U.N.'s whims. Resources, which are fundamental for survival and progress, could be used as leverage, dangled as a carrot, or withheld as a stick.

Imagine a scenario where a nation resists a particular U.N. directive. In retaliation, they might find their energy resources curtailed, leading to blackouts, or their food resources slashed, leading to starvation. This isn't just about economic repercussions; it's about the very survival of nations and their citizens.

Furthermore, such centralized control might stifle innovation and competition. If resources are allocated by a single entity's discretion, what incentive is there for nations to innovate, strive for efficiency, or compete in the global marketplace? The spirit of entrepreneurship, which has driven human progress for centuries, could be dampened.

In conclusion, while the U.N.'s supposed advantage in resource allocation speaks of a world united in purpose and fairness, the dangers of such a model are stark. With no checks and balances, nations could find themselves at the mercy of a singular entity, leading to a potential dystopia where dissent is not only silenced but punished through the very essence of survival – resources.

Economic Leverage:

The economic arena is a pivotal battleground for dominance and power. Over centuries, nations have risen and fallen based on the might of their economies. With globalization, the intricacies and interdependencies have only grown, and so has the desire for a more streamlined, unified system. However, can a singular entity, like the U.N., truly manage and wield the diverse economic levers of the world without causing more harm than good?

- **Supposed Advantage:** The allure of a unified economic system, in theory, is undeniable. Trade wars, which can lead to staggering losses and collateral damage, would be a thing of the past. Currency wars, which often destabilize economies and lead to catastrophic financial fallout, would be negated. No longer would nations have to navigate the complex web of international tariffs, trade barriers, and economic sanctions. An overarching economic authority could streamline processes, eliminate redundancies, and ensure a more collaborative global marketplace. Theories propose that such consolidation could lead to reduced transaction costs, improved efficiencies, and a more predictable economic environment for investors and businesses alike.

Additionally, in a unified system, economic crises in one region could be swiftly addressed by pooling resources from more prosperous areas. No longer would nations suffer in isolation, as a global safety net would be in place.

- **Negative Side:** However, this rosy picture glosses over the immense challenges and dangers of economic homogenization. Every nation, with its unique cultural, geographical, and historical background, has developed its own economic systems, policies, and practices. These have evolved over centuries, finely tuned to the needs, aspirations, and challenges of their people.

By imposing a one-size-fits-all economic model, we risk causing catastrophic disruptions. For instance, a policy that boosts the economy in one region might decimate another. Consider the intricacies of agricultural subsidies: what benefits a farming community in Asia might wreak havoc in Africa.

Furthermore, economic autonomy is crucial for nations to adapt to changing scenarios. In a centralized system, nations might be forced to adhere to policies that are clearly detrimental to them but benefit the larger collective. This could lead to widespread economic disparity. Richer nations or regions might prosper even more, while the poorer ones could fall into deeper economic despair, unable to break free due to the shackles of the unified system.

Also, in times of global economic downturns, the lack of diversified economic systems means there's no buffer. A crisis in one part of the system could rapidly cascade through the entire global economic structure.

Lastly, economic power equates to political power. If the U.N. controls the world's economy, it effectively controls its politics. Nations might find themselves reduced to mere administrative regions, their voices silenced, their unique challenges unheard, and their autonomy stripped away.

In essence, while a unified economic system under the U.N.'s dominion promises stability and collaboration, the potential fallout is staggering. Economic diversity, just like biodiversity, is a strength, not a weakness. The price of homogenization could be a loss of national identity, autonomy, and the right to self-determination.

Conflict Resolution:

History has been marred with conflicts, from border skirmishes to full-blown world wars. One of the foundational principles upon which the United Nations was formed post World War II was to prevent another such cataclysmic event. But as we gaze into the potential future where the U.N. takes a central role in governance, we must question: does centralized conflict resolution truly offer the panacea it promises or does it introduce a new set of perils?

- **Supposed Advantage:** A single global government, in theory, has the potential to resolve conflicts with a swiftness and clarity that the current fragmented political landscape cannot. By removing the layers of bureaucracy, national interests, and geopolitics, decisions could be reached more promptly, ideally preventing minor disagreements from escalating into major confrontations. Such a structure could oversee the disarmament of warring factions, mediate disputes impartially, and ensure a quicker return to peace.

  Moreover, a centralized authority would possess a holistic view of global issues, potentially enabling it to identify and address root causes of conflicts, be they economic disparities, resource shortages, or cultural misunderstandings. The sheer might of a singular global entity could also deter parties from engaging in aggressive actions, knowing the full weight of global governance would be against them.

- **Negative Side:** However, beneath this utopian veneer lies a series of treacherous pitfalls. To begin with, the notion of a single entity resolving conflicts assumes that this body is inherently unbiased and altruistic. Realistically, any governing body, no matter how global, would have its own set of interests, biases, and agendas. The decision-making, then, might not truly be for the greater good, but for the preservation and furthering of the elite governing class.

Take, for instance, a scenario where a region revolts against economic policies that it finds oppressive. In a world dominated by the U.N., this dissenting region could be painted as a rogue state, and its legitimate concerns might be silenced or dismissed. Without checks and balances from other sovereign nations, there's little to stop the global governing body from enforcing its will, however tyrannical.

Furthermore, centralized conflict resolution risks simplifying and homogenizing deeply complex regional issues. Conflicts often arise from intricate historical, cultural, and socio-political contexts. A one-size-fits-all approach might overlook these nuances, leading to solutions that don't address the root causes, or worse, exacerbate them.

Lastly, the absence of a countervailing force means there's no balance of power. Traditionally, the balance of power between nations has been a crucial factor in maintaining global peace. But in a centralized world, oppressed groups or regions would lack international allies to champion their cause. Their voices could be easily muffled, their plights overlooked, and their oppressions intensified.

In sum, while the idea of a centralized conflict resolution mechanism seems appealing, it carries with it grave risks. The lack of diversity in decision-making, potential biases of the governing elite, and absence of international checks and balances might not lead to a peaceful utopia but a world rife with silent sufferings and unheard cries for justice.

Unified Response to Global Issues:

As the world becomes increasingly interconnected, the ripple effects of major global events are felt far and wide. Natural disasters, pandemics, and economic downturns in one part of the world can impact the livelihoods of people continents away. In such a landscape, the idea of a unified response to these colossal challenges seems not only enticing but essential. Yet, delving deeper, we find the terrain fraught with complications and unintended consequences.

- **Supposed Advantage:** A unified response under the leadership of a single governing entity like the U.N. paints a picture of efficiency and coherence. Instead of multiple nations scrambling, often with conflicting strategies, a singular authoritative body could orchestrate a coordinated, large-scale response.

  Imagine, for instance, the outbreak of a new deadly virus. A centralized authority could mobilize resources, streamline research, ensure consistent messaging, and execute a uniform containment strategy. Similarly, with an issue as vast and urgent as climate change, having a united front might ensure that measures are taken on a global scale, with resources and efforts pooled to tackle the most pressing environmental challenges.

  Additionally, with a single governing entity, there would be fewer bureaucratic hurdles. Decisions could be made swiftly, without the need for lengthy negotiations between countries, leading to rapid action in crisis situations.

- **Negative Side:** While the idea of a unified strategy is beguiling in its simplicity, it's here that the devil truly is in the details. A single strategy, no matter how well-intentioned, risks overlooking the nuances and intricacies of individual regions and communities.

For instance, a global strategy to combat climate change might prioritize reducing carbon emissions. While this is a noble goal, it could result in stringent measures that cripple industries in developing nations, where millions depend on them for their livelihood. Meanwhile, developed countries, which historically have been the larger contributors to carbon emissions, might find loopholes to maintain their industrial superiority. Such a monolithic approach would exacerbate existing inequalities, further entrenching the divide between the "haves" and the "have-nots."

Furthermore, a centralized approach could stifle innovation. Different regions have unique challenges and might come up with innovative, localized solutions when given the autonomy to do so. However, with a top-down, one-size-fits-all strategy, such regional ingenuity might be stifled or overlooked.

Moreover, decisions taken by a centralized body are susceptible to biases and might disproportionately favor regions or groups that wield more influence within the governing entity. Marginalized communities, with lesser representation or say, might find their concerns and needs sidelined. They could be subjected to policies that are detrimental to their well-being, with little recourse for redress.

In essence, while the allure of a unified response to global challenges is undeniable, the risks associated with such a centralized approach are significant. The mosaic of our world, with its rich tapestry of cultures, histories, and challenges, demands solutions that are as diverse and multifaceted as its problems. Anything less runs the risk of deepening divisions and amplifying sufferings.

Cultural Homogenization:

The idea of a global community, united in its beliefs, customs, and values, is a tantalizing vision for many. Such a world, devoid of cultural clashes and misunderstandings, might seem like a utopia where harmony reigns. But like all visions, this too has its shadows, its overlooked corners where the darkness gathers, hinting at complexities that a cursory glance might miss.

- **Supposed Advantage:** At its core, the idea of a globally unified culture stems from the noble intention of fostering unity and mutual understanding. Cultural clashes have been at the heart of many historical conflicts. By streamlining cultural values and norms, proponents argue that misunderstandings could be minimized.

  Imagine a world where there are no language barriers, where every individual understands and abides by a universal set of values, and where cultural faux pas are things of the past. This could, theoretically, lead to more effective communication and collaboration on global issues. Business negotiations would become more streamlined, diplomacy might face fewer roadblocks, and individuals could traverse the globe without the fear of inadvertently offending their hosts.

- **Negative Side:** However, the concept of cultural homogenization, when examined critically, seems more dystopian than utopian. For starters, culture is not just a set of random customs and rituals; it's the very fabric of a community's history, struggles, triumphs, and collective memory. The process of homogenizing cultures, therefore, would essentially mean erasing millennia of rich histories and lived experiences.

Moreover, the diversity of cultures across the globe is not just about different cuisines, languages, or clothing. It's also about diverse ways of thinking, problem-solving, and innovating. The diverse cultural backgrounds have historically been crucibles for groundbreaking innovations. For instance, ancient civilizations like the Greeks, Chinese, Mayans, and Egyptians, each with their distinct cultures, contributed uniquely to fields such as science, mathematics, architecture, and philosophy. Imagine if all these cultures had been homogenized into one. Would Archimedes, Confucius, and Imhotep have had the same insights and breakthroughs? It's unlikely.

Additionally, the process of enforcing a global culture implies a body that decides what this culture should encompass. And here lies a significant danger. Who decides which values, languages, and customs make the cut? Such decisions are likely to be influenced by the dominant powers within the governing entity, leading to a culture that mirrors their values and priorities. Consequently, minority cultures, especially those from marginalized or less influential regions, face the risk of being entirely obliterated.

In a homogenized world, future generations might grow up in a cultural vacuum, devoid of the rich tapestry of tales, music, art, and wisdom that diverse cultures offer. Such a world might be more cohesive, but it would also be less colorful, less vibrant, and, most importantly, less human.

In conclusion, while the allure of a unified global culture might seem appealing on the surface, the costs—both tangible and intangible—are immense. The diversity of human cultures is a testament to our species' adaptability, creativity, and resilience. Efforts to streamline it, no matter how well-intentioned, could stifle the very essence of what it means to be human.

Other Disadvantages to the UN in Achieving Global Dominance:

Totalitarian Concerns:

Historically, the idea of a centralized, singular authority has been met with both fascination and apprehension. On one hand, it promises unity, uniformity, and a streamlined approach to governance. On the other, it presents the harrowing specter of unchecked power and the potential loss of individual freedoms.

With centralized dominance, the UN might be seen not just as a global authority, but as a totalitarian regime.

Such fears aren't unfounded. The annals of history are littered with examples of centralized authorities that began with the noblest of intentions but quickly descended into oppressive regimes. From the Roman Empire's despotic rulers to the more recent authoritarian governments in the 20th century, the world has witnessed how absolute power can corrupt absolutely. A global body with unchecked power could easily morph into an oppressive force, trampling over individual rights and freedoms in the name of broader objectives.

This could stoke fears of authoritarianism and result in widespread resistance.

The very essence of democracy is the distribution of power and the checks and balances that prevent its concentration. A global body with dominance would fly in the face of this principle, and would likely be seen as a threat to democratic ideals. The result? Widespread resistance, not just from nations but from individuals who cherish their freedoms and autonomy.

Operational Overwhelm:

Governing is one thing; dominating is entirely another. The intricacies of global governance, even without the intent of dominance, are complex enough.

Dominating rather than governing means the UN would have to enforce its authority in every member nation, dealing with resistances, uprisings, and possibly even rebellions.

The logistics alone would be a nightmare. The UN would need to establish mechanisms to monitor and control the internal affairs of every member nation. This would require a massive bureaucracy, expansive surveillance systems, and possibly even a global policing force. Beyond this, the UN would have to contend with local nuances, cultural differences, and regional sentiments, which could further complicate enforcement.

Resistance from All Nations:

It's naive to assume that only powerful nations would resist a global dominant force. History has shown that even smaller states, driven by national pride and a desire for sovereignty, can mount formidable resistance.

Not just powerful nations, but even smaller states and non-state actors would push back against a body attempting global dominance, leading to potential widespread conflict.

Every nation, regardless of its size, has a unique cultural, historical, and political identity. The idea of ceding control to a global entity would be anathema to many. Even non-state actors, such as indigenous communities, regional groups, and other organizations, would likely rally against what they'd perceive as an external threat to their autonomy. This could lead to guerilla warfare, civil unrest, and widespread instability.

The ripple effects of such resistance would be manifold. The global economy could be disrupted, leading to recessions or even depressions. Humanitarian crises might arise as a result of conflicts and resistances. And the very fabric of international cooperation could be torn apart.

While the idea of a centralized global authority might seem appealing in terms of efficiency and uniformity, the practical implications and potential consequences paint a grim picture. The challenges of enforcing dominance, the inevitable resistances, and the overarching fears of totalitarianism suggest that such a path would be fraught with peril.

Economic Homogenization:

The push towards a single global economy under a dominant UN regime raises significant concerns. While the concept of a unified global economy has its merits in theory, the practical implications are far more complicated and potentially damaging.

Instead of disparities, there might be attempts to create a single global economy.

In a world where economies are as diverse as the cultures and societies they spring from, a one-size-fits-all economic model is not just impractical, but it can be catastrophic. For instance, policies suited to advanced economies might wreak havoc in developing ones, destroying local industries and livelihoods.

While this sounds beneficial, it might destroy local economies, causing more harm than good.

Local economies with unique characteristics could be bulldozed by homogenous economic policies, leading to job losses, economic monocultures, and the collapse of small and medium enterprises. This would not only harm local industries but also exacerbate unemployment and poverty.

Cultural Erasure:

The cultural implications of a globally dominant UN are profound and deeply troubling. Culture, with its myriad expressions, is the bedrock of a society's identity and heritage.

Dominance would likely involve more aggressive attempts to homogenize cultures.

In a bid to create a streamlined, globally cohesive society, unique cultural practices, languages, and traditions could be pushed aside. The world might witness a cultural flattening, where diverse expressions are replaced by a singular, dominant culture.

This could lead to a loss of cultural identities and heritage.

The erasure of cultural diversity would not only mean the loss of colorful traditions and languages but also the disappearance of centuries of knowledge, art, and ways of life. This could lead to a homogenized, monotonous world devoid of the richness that diverse cultures bring.

Unprecedented Scrutiny:

In an era where information is as fluid as it is pervasive, the actions of a dominant global body like the UN would be under constant and intense scrutiny.

Beyond regular scrutiny, there'd be a global narrative painting the UN as potential oppressors.

Every move and decision made by the UN would be analyzed, criticized, and debated. In the digital age, where news spreads instantaneously, any perceived overstep would fuel global dissent.

This would be amplified in the age of digital media and instant communication.

Social media platforms, blogs, and online forums would become hotbeds of discussion and dissent against the UN. In such an environment, maintaining legitimacy and trust would be a significant challenge for the UN, potentially leading to widespread public disillusionment and resistance.

The aspiration for global dominance by the UN, while aimed at creating a unified world, brings with it a host of concerns that cannot be ignored. The threat to local economies, the potential erasure of rich cultural diversities, and the heightened global scrutiny in an interconnected world pose significant challenges. These issues highlight the need for a balanced approach that respects national sovereignty, cultural diversity, and economic independence.

Collapse of National Systems:

The pursuit of global dominance by the United Nations could precipitate the gradual disintegration of national systems and governance structures. This aspect carries profound implications for global stability and individual nation-state identities.

Dominance could lead to the dissolution of national systems and structures.

Such a centralized approach to global governance could result in the erosion of national institutions, including legislative bodies, judicial systems, and local governance structures. The diverse and context-specific systems that currently address the unique needs of different populations might be replaced by a monolithic, one-size-fits-all approach, potentially leading to inefficiencies and unaddressed local issues.

While some might see this as advantageous, it also means that if the UN system fails, there's nothing to fall back on.

In a scenario where the central system encounters a crisis or failure, the lack of robust national systems to fall back on could lead to chaos and disorder. The absence of local governance structures and mechanisms would leave populations vulnerable and exposed to the risks of systemic failures at a global level.

Potential for Tyranny:

With centralized control comes the increased risk of authoritarian governance, where the central authority's decisions might no longer align with the welfare of the global populace.

The risk of corruption evolves into the risk of tyranny, where decisions are no longer made for global good but for maintaining dominance.

In such a scenario, the central authority could prioritize its survival and control over the actual needs and welfare of the people. Decision-making might become more about preserving power and less about addressing global challenges, leading to oppressive and tyrannical governance.

Dissolution of Consensus:

A critical aspect of global governance is the building of consensus among diverse nations. However, in a scenario of global dominance, this democratic principle could be significantly undermined.

Consensus might become a thing of the past. Instead, decisions could be made by a central authority, diminishing the voices of many.

This shift would mean that the varied perspectives and voices of different nations, cultures, and groups would no longer play a significant role in global decision-making. Instead, a centralized authority would make unilateral decisions, potentially disregarding the diverse needs and concerns of the global community. The loss of a consensus-driven approach could lead to discontent and disillusionment among member states, further destabilizing the global order.

The quest for global dominance by the UN, as proposed in this critical analysis, carries with it the risks of collapsing national systems, potential tyranny, and the dissolution of consensus-based decision-making. These factors combined pose significant threats to global stability, democratic governance, and the respect for diverse perspectives and needs.

Conclusion

The concept of the United Nations pursuing global dominance marks a significant divergence from the foundational ethos upon which it was established. This notion, explored throughout the chapter, raises not only practical challenges but also profound ethical and moral questions.

The pursuit of global dominance presents a stark contrast to the UN's original charter and principles.

The United Nations was founded on the principles of promoting peace, fostering international cooperation, and ensuring respect for human rights. However, the pursuit of global dominance, as critiqued in this chapter, deviates markedly from these founding ideals. It introduces a paradigm where power and control supersede collaboration and mutual respect among nations. Such a shift could potentially transform the UN from a platform for collective action and dialogue into a centralized authority with far-reaching influence over sovereign nations.

The challenges and concerns of such a scenario are not just practical but deeply ethical and moral.

The implications of a single entity exerting dominance over diverse nations extend beyond logistical and operational concerns. They delve into the realm of moral and ethical considerations. Issues such as the erosion of national sovereignty, cultural homogenization, and the suppression of dissent challenge the core values of democracy, freedom, and self-determination. The ethical dilemma posed by such a concentration of power raises questions about the legitimacy and morality of imposing a singular vision upon a multifaceted global populace.

While unity is a noble aspiration, dominance carries the risk of oppression.

Unity and cooperation among nations are laudable goals that the UN has strived to achieve. However, unity that morphs into dominance risks becoming oppressive. The transition from cooperative decision-making to unilateral dictates under the guise of global governance could lead to a loss of diversity in thought, policy, and culture, stifling innovation and progress. The risk of authoritarianism looms large in such a scenario, where dissenting voices might be silenced, and minority interests overlooked.

It will be the collective responsibility of the global community to ensure that power, in whatever form it exists, remains in check.

In conclusion, the notion of the UN pursuing global dominance requires critical scrutiny and vigilance. It is the collective responsibility of the international community, including nation-states, non-governmental organizations, civil society, and individuals, to ensure that any form of power—be it economic, political, or cultural—is exercised with restraint, transparency, and accountability. The preservation of a balanced, fair, and equitable global order depends on the continuous oversight and active engagement of the global populace, ensuring that the ideals of democracy, diversity, and mutual respect remain at the forefront of international governance.

Chapter 11
The Shadow Partners

<u>International Organizations Aligned with the U.N.'s Quest for Dominance</u>

In the intricate web of international relations, organizations operate in tandem, often presenting an image of cooperation for global welfare. However, skeptics argue that behind this facade lies a more sinister agenda - that of global dominance. This chapter unveils the international organizations often touted as the U.N.'s covert partners in their alleged quest for world dominance.

International Monetary Fund (IMF) and World Bank: The Power Brokers

In the vast landscape of international organizations, few wield as much influence as the International Monetary Fund (IMF) and the World Bank. These financial giants are frequently perceived as the linchpins in the U.N.'s alleged quest for global dominance, a theory that gains traction when scrutinized through a critical lens.

Alleged Role in Global Dominance: The IMF and the World Bank, according to critics, function as more than mere financial institutions. They are seen as instrumental in shaping the economic and political landscapes of developing countries. Through their substantial lending capabilities, these organizations are accused of enforcing economic policies and reforms that align closely with what is deemed beneficial for the global agenda set by the U.N. and its most influential member states. This influence extends beyond mere financial assistance, embedding itself into the very fabric of a nation's policy-making process.

Benefits for the Power Structure: By keeping nations financially dependent, the IMF and World Bank are in a position to dictate terms that go beyond simple economic advice. This leverage ensures that policies and reforms favorable to the interests of these institutions and their most powerful backers are adopted and implemented. This creates a cycle of dependence where countries are compelled to align with these global directives to ensure continued financial support, thus extending the influence of these institutions.

The Reality Check: While it's undeniable that the IMF and World Bank have a significant impact on the economies of nations, especially those in the developing world, the assertion that their primary objective is global dominance sparks heated debate. Detractors argue that these institutions, under the guise of fostering economic stability and development, might be pursuing a more covert agenda of influencing and reshaping global political and economic structures. This contention raises serious questions about the true motivations behind the actions and policies of these influential financial entities.

In conclusion, the role of the IMF and the World Bank in the international arena is complex and multifaceted. While they undoubtedly possess the power to influence nations and shape global economic trends, the extent to which this power is wielded for the purpose of achieving global dominance remains a topic of intense scrutiny and debate. What is clear is that their actions have far-reaching implications, not just for the economies they interact with, but for the broader geopolitical landscape.

World Health Organization (WHO):

Alleged Role in Global Domination: The World Health Organization, as an influential arm of the U.N. in public health, is perceived by some as playing a crucial role in furthering the U.N.'s global ambitions. Conspiracy theorists assert that WHO's policies and guidelines are not just about promoting health but are tactically used to steer global population dynamics and health decisions. This, they argue, is part of a broader strategy to establish control over national health agendas, aligning them with a universal narrative that suits the interests of those seeking global dominance.

Benefits of Health Control: Dominating the sphere of global health grants unparalleled leverage. Control over health guidelines and policies translates to significant influence over the internal affairs of nations. In times of health emergencies, such as pandemics, this influence becomes even more pronounced. The ability to dictate how countries respond to health crises, what measures they implement, and how they allocate resources, effectively puts the WHO in a position to sway national policies and economic decisions. This level of influence can have profound implications for national sovereignty and decision-making autonomy.

The Reality Check: While the WHO's role and influence in global health matters are undeniable, the notion that it operates with the primary intent of global dominance is heavily contested. Critics of the WHO point to its response to events like the COVID-19 pandemic as evidence of its disproportionate influence and alleged mismanagement. However, it's important to recognize that the WHO's vast majority of operations and initiatives are geared towards enhancing global health, combatting diseases, and improving healthcare access and quality worldwide. The debate over the WHO's intentions and actions remains a complex and nuanced one, reflecting the challenges of managing health on a global scale.

In summary, the World Health Organization's standing as a key player in international health brings with it both immense responsibility and scrutiny. While its actions and decisions significantly impact global health policies and practices, the narrative of it being a tool for U.N.-led global dominance is a subject of ongoing debate and skepticism, underscoring the need for a balanced and critical examination of its role in the international arena.

World Trade Organization (WTO):

Alleged Role in Global Economic Manipulation: The World Trade Organization, as per the suspicions of critical theorists, is seen as a major chess piece in the U.N.'s strategy for economic control. By dictating international trade rules and regulations, the WTO is believed to possess the capability to steer global markets. This power, in the eyes of skeptics, aligns closely with the U.N.'s objectives, allowing for a coordinated approach to shape and direct global economies. The assertion is that this control extends beyond mere market dynamics, potentially influencing political and economic decisions at the national level.

Benefits of Trade Control: The control of international trade is a potent tool. By dictating trade policies, tariffs, and agreements, the WTO can create economic dependencies and imbalances. This control, critics argue, will lead to certain countries becoming increasingly reliant on others, effectively creating a hierarchy in global economics. Nations, particularly those in the developing world, might find themselves compelled to comply with directives that align with the interests of more dominant players, thus perpetuating a cycle of dependency and influence.

The Reality Check: While it's undeniable that the WTO plays a significant role in global trade, the notion of it being an instrument of U.N.-led global dominance is contentious. The WTO's decision-making process is based on a consensus model, involving all member states. This model, while not without its power imbalances, suggests a more complex and nuanced reality than a simple narrative of domination. Critics often point to instances where trade regulations have disproportionately favored wealthier nations to support claims of bias. However, it's essential to recognize the organization's fundamental role in facilitating international trade and resolving disputes, a far cry from the sweeping control implied by theories of global dominance.

In this light, the World Trade Organization's function in the global landscape is multifaceted. While it wields significant influence over trade policies and can impact economies worldwide, the extent to which this translates into a deliberate strategy for global dominance is subject to interpretation and debate. The complexities and intricacies of international trade make it a realm where power, influence, and interests intersect, often leading to contested perspectives on the role and intentions of pivotal organizations like the WTO.

Non-Governmental Organizations (NGOs):

Alleged Role in Promoting U.N. Agendas: In the critical discourse surrounding global governance, a recurrent theme is the role of Non-Governmental Organizations. There is a growing suspicion among skeptics that numerous high-profile NGOs, heavily funded by global elites, are covertly working to bolster the United Nations' aspirations for global dominance. These NGOs, it is argued, are not mere independent entities driven by altruistic goals but are instrumental in subtly weaving the U.N.'s dominance narrative into various societal fabrics. They are seen as crucial players in a grander scheme, cloaked under the veil of philanthropy and social welfare.

Benefits of Grassroots Influence: The strategic advantage of employing NGOs lies in their grassroots-level operation. They can effectively infiltrate local communities, influencing narratives and shaping public opinion to align with the U.N.'s broader global initiatives. This influence extends beyond mere advocacy; it involves the mobilization of public sentiment, lobbying for policy changes, and sometimes even intervening in local governance structures. Their reach and impact on the ground level could be a significant lever in swaying socio-political landscapes to mirror U.N. directives.

The Reality Check: It is essential, however, to approach this narrative with a degree of skepticism. While it is true that some NGOs have faced criticism for their agendas, biases, and sources of funding, it is a gross oversimplification to categorize all NGOs under this sweeping generalization. Many NGOs worldwide operate with a genuine commitment to societal betterment, addressing issues ranging from poverty and education to environmental conservation. They often fill gaps left by governmental inaction and are vital in bringing neglected issues to the forefront. To label all NGOs as mere pawns in a global game of dominance is to overlook the nuanced and often complex realities of their operations and contributions.

The discourse around NGOs as purported shadow partners in the U.N.'s quest for dominance taps into broader concerns about the influence of non-state actors in global politics. It underscores the need for transparency, accountability, and critical examination of the motives and impacts of these organizations in the tapestry of international relations. While acknowledging the potential for manipulation and hidden agendas, it is also crucial to recognize the multifaceted roles that NGOs play in addressing global challenges and contributing to the welfare of communities worldwide.

Multinational Corporations:

Alleged Role in Global Scheme: In the complex tapestry of global politics and economics, multinational corporations, particularly those in the technology and pharmaceutical sectors, are frequently cast in a contentious light. Critics assert that these corporate behemoths are not mere profit-driven entities but are, in fact, key players in the United Nations' alleged agenda for global dominance. The narrative posits that these corporations are deeply entwined with the U.N.'s initiatives, covertly working to mold a world order that is inherently favorable to their sprawling business empires. They are portrayed as the unseen hands guiding policies and decisions, orchestrating events to carve a global landscape that is conducive to their continued growth and influence.

Benefits of Corporate-Global Alignment: The purported symbiosis between these multinational giants and the U.N. yields significant benefits for the former. By aligning with global directives, these corporations stand to solidify their market dominance on a global scale. This alignment might manifest in various forms - from influencing international regulatory frameworks to favor their technologies, to championing global health initiatives that boost their pharmaceutical sales. In essence, the collaboration is seen as a strategic move to squash competition and create a monopolistic stronghold under the guise of supporting U.N. goals.

The Reality Check: While it is irrefutable that multinational corporations wield considerable influence in shaping international policies and economic trends, the claim that they uniformly conspire with the U.N. to achieve global dominance requires a more nuanced examination. The relationship between these corporations and international bodies like the U.N. is complex and multifaceted. Many corporations do engage in activities aligned with U.N. objectives, ranging from sustainable development to technological innovation for social good. However, to paint all multinational corporations with the same brush of conspiratorial collusion oversimplifies the diversity of corporate motives and actions. It also neglects the instances where corporate interests have clashed with U.N. directives or where corporations have acted independently of any U.N. influence.

In summary, the narrative of multinational corporations as shadow partners in the U.N.'s supposed quest for global dominance taps into broader debates about corporate influence in international affairs. While it is crucial to scrutinize and critique the role of these powerful entities in shaping global policies and practices, it is equally important to recognize the varied and complex nature of their engagement with international bodies and agendas. The relationship between the U.N. and multinational corporations is not a monolithic alliance but a dynamic interplay of interests, influences, and objectives that deserve careful and critical analysis.

In Conclusion

As we draw the curtain on this investigation, it's evident that the United Nations, augmented by its sprawling array of partners, stands at the epicenter of formidable global influence. The intricate web spun by this nexus of power, wealth, and strategic alliances is unmistakable, casting long shadows over the geopolitical landscape. Yet, the portrayal of the U.N. and its affiliates as covert architects of a world order marked by domination and subjugation remains a deeply contentious and polarizing narrative.

The allegations of secret agendas and global control, while gripping, often overlook the nuanced realities of international diplomacy and governance. It's imperative to approach these assertions with a critical eye, recognizing the potential for sensationalism and oversimplification in such sweeping claims. However, this does not absolve the United Nations and its partners of accountability; their actions and motivations must be continually scrutinized and challenged, ensuring that their influence does not overstep into realms of coercion or undermine the sovereignty of nations.

In this complex dance of power, it is the responsibility of the global citizenry to remain informed, engaged, and critical. The pursuit of a more equitable and peaceful world is a noble endeavor, but it must not be pursued blindly or at the cost of individual freedoms and national autonomy. The U.N.'s role, along with its network of partners, must be persistently examined to ensure that their collective impact aligns with the principles of justice, equality, and true global cooperation, rather than veering towards a surreptitious consolidation of power.

In essence, while we acknowledge the potential for overreach and the need for vigilance, we must also recognize the complexity of global governance and the myriad challenges it faces. The narrative of the U.N. as a monolithic entity bent on global domination is an oversimplification of a far more intricate and multifaceted reality. As such, our analysis and critique must be balanced, informed, and devoid of reductionism, keeping in mind the ultimate goal of a world where every nation and individual can thrive in harmony and dignity.

Chapter 12
Solutions and Alternatives

<u>Proposed Reforms for the UN</u>

Short of shutting down the U.N. completely, these are the minimum requirements needed to reform an institution that many view as teetering on the brink of global dominance, while masquerading as a harbinger of global peace.

Decentralization of Power:

Historical Context: The creation of the UN, specifically the Security Council with its P5 veto powers, was originally designed as a safeguard against the horrors of another world war. However, in today's context, this arrangement is archaic and out of touch. It's increasingly seen as a mechanism that allows certain powers to control global narratives and enforce policies that serve their interests, rather than those of the global community.

Suggested Reforms: The archaic structure of the Security Council demands an overhaul. A rotational system for permanent membership, including countries from historically underrepresented regions, is crucial. This would bring diverse perspectives to the table and prevent a few nations from dictating global policies. Moreover, the veto power needs a radical reformation - either its complete elimination or at the very least, a system where multiple vetoes are required to block a resolution. This would mitigate the current scenario where a single nation's objection can paralyze decision-making.

Potential Outcomes: Such decentralization is more than a power shuffle; it's a necessary step towards democratizing the UN. It would mitigate the risk of the institution being used as a tool by powerful nations to further their geopolitical ambitions. More equitable decision-making could restore faith in the UN as an institution genuinely committed to collective global welfare rather than serving as a puppet to dominant countries.

These reforms are not merely a checklist but a call for a fundamental shift in how the UN operates. By addressing these critical areas, the UN can transition from an entity perceived as an instrument of control and dominance to one that truly embodies the ideals of democracy, fairness, and representation. This is not just a reform; it's a radical reimagining of the UN's role in the 21st century and beyond.

Enhanced Transparency:

In confronting the United Nations' perceived trajectory towards global dominance, it is crucial to instigate reforms that will unequivocally alter its modus operandi. Beyond decentralizing power, the next crucial step is enhancing transparency - a move essential to peel back layers of secrecy that currently shroud the UN's operations.

Behind Closed Doors: The UN's current operational framework is plagued by a disturbing lack of transparency. High-stakes meetings and negotiations, pivotal in shaping global policies, often occur out of the public eye. This breeds suspicion and fosters conspiracy theories, painting the UN as a shadowy figure orchestrating global events to its benefit.

Suggested Reforms: To counter this narrative, a radical shift towards openness is non-negotiable. This means broadcasting all sessions live, except those involving sensitive national security matters. Crucial documents, decisions, internal communications, and financial dealings must be open to public scrutiny. The UN must embrace an open-source ethos, allowing global citizens to engage directly in non-sensitive discussions, fostering a sense of inclusion and participatory governance.

Potential Outcomes: Such unprecedented transparency will serve as a potent antidote to conspiracy theories and allegations of clandestine agendas. It would demonstrate the UN's commitment to global cooperation and accountability. By laying its operations open for the world to see, the UN can rebuild trust, legitimizing its role as a global facilitator rather than a covert operator.

These reforms are not just about appeasing critics or silencing conspiracy theories. They are about fundamentally redefining the United Nations' engagement with the world it seeks to serve. By adopting these reforms, the UN can shed its image as a potential global overlord and reaffirm its position as a transparent, accountable, and truly democratic institution. This transformation is crucial not just for the UN's survival but for the future of global governance as we know it.

Accountability Mechanisms:

Impunity Concerns: Currently, the United Nations and its various branches are cloaked in diplomatic immunity, which, while necessary for independent operation, has inadvertently created a shield against accountability. This protection has been misinterpreted by some as a license to operate without fear of repercussions, even in cases of significant missteps or overreach. The perception that the UN could potentially err without facing consequences fuels the narrative of it being an untouchable entity, potentially inching towards unchecked global dominance.

Suggested Reforms: To dismantle this image of invulnerability, the establishment of an independent judiciary body is imperative. This entity must stand apart from the UN's influence, serving as an impartial adjudicator of the organization's actions. It would provide a platform for grievances against the UN, be it from member states or impacted populations, to be fairly addressed. Alongside, instituting a system of periodic reviews involving a diverse committee - comprising member states, non-governmental organizations, and representatives from global civil society - is crucial. This committee would function as a watchdog, evaluating the UN's actions and policies, ensuring they align with global expectations and norms.

Potential Outcomes: The introduction of these accountability mechanisms would signal a seismic shift in the UN's operational ethos. It would transform the organization from a perceived untouchable behemoth into a transparent and accountable entity. Such a structure would not only serve as a check against the misuse of power but also instill a culture of responsibility and caution within the UN. By knowing that every action could be scrutinized and judged, the UN would likely adopt a more circumspect approach, aligning its actions more closely with the principles of fairness and justice it champions.

These reforms are vital in recalibrating the UN's trajectory. They are not just about damage control or appeasing critics but about fundamentally reshaping the organization into one that is more attuned to the ideals of justice, transparency, and accountability. The implementation of these reforms would not only restore faith in the UN but also fortify its role as a true servant of the global community.

In Conclusion

As it stands, the United Nations finds itself at a pivotal crossroads, facing increasing scrutiny and skepticism about its role and influence in global affairs. This call for comprehensive reforms transcends mere reaction to conspiracy theories; it embodies a profound and urgent demand for the institution to fundamentally reassess and recalibrate its approach and mechanisms. The global community is in dire need of a cooperative international body, one that not only spearheads collective efforts for a better world but also does so while meticulously respecting and preserving the unique identities, sovereignties, and aspirations of its diverse member states.

The choice facing the UN is stark and consequential. It can either respond proactively to these calls for change, embracing a path of transformation and renewal, thereby reinforcing its legitimacy and effectiveness, or it can continue on its current trajectory. The latter risks solidifying an image of the UN as an out-of-touch, overly centralized entity, increasingly alienated from the very nations and peoples it seeks to represent and assist.

In essence, the UN's future relevance, effectiveness, and trustworthiness hinge on its willingness and ability to reform. The organization must evolve into a truly representative and accountable entity, one that is perceived not as a looming specter of global dominance but as a beacon of collaborative, equitable, and just governance. The global community's trust and the UN's own legacy depend on its response to this defining challenge.

Alternatives to the Current Global Cooperation Model

As the concerns surrounding the United Nations and its purported push for global dominance intensify, the dialogue around alternative structures of international collaboration has taken center stage. The foundation of these alternatives is rooted in decentralizing global authority and placing more emphasis on structures that are more connected to regional and issue-specific realities. Let's delve deeper into these alternatives:

Regional Alliances:

Historical Precedence: The role of regional alliances has been crucial throughout history. Entities like the European Union and the African Union have demonstrated the potential of regional cohesion. These alliances, formed in the aftermath of conflicts or to address shared regional concerns, have shown how localized cooperation can foster stability and growth.

Advantages: One of the most significant benefits of regional alliances is their inherent understanding of the local context. These bodies are more attuned to the specific needs, challenges, and dynamics of their regions. Unlike a global behemoth like the UN, regional alliances can offer nuanced, culturally sensitive, and relevant solutions. They also promote regional integration, strengthening economic and political ties and fostering a sense of community and shared destiny among member nations. In cases of conflict resolution, regional alliances can mediate with a deeper understanding of the underlying issues, often more effectively than a distant international body.

Potential Challenges: However, the reliance on regional alliances isn't without its pitfalls. There's a real danger of regional power imbalances, where dominant nations within these alliances could wield disproportionate influence, overshadowing the interests of smaller or less powerful members. This could lead to regional hegemonies, potentially replicating the power dynamics criticized within the UN. Moreover, there's the risk of regionalism leading to isolationism. Focused on their immediate vicinity, these alliances might neglect broader global responsibilities, leading to fragmented international relations. In extreme scenarios, this fragmentation could escalate into inter-regional tensions or conflicts, particularly in areas where resources are contested or where political and ideological divides run deep.

Balancing Act: To counter these challenges, it's crucial to establish checks and balances within regional alliances. Clear guidelines on decision-making processes, equitable representation, and conflict resolution mechanisms can help mitigate the risks of dominance by a single nation. Additionally, fostering inter-regional dialogues and cooperation can ensure that while regions address their specific needs, they also remain integrated into the broader global community. This approach would involve a delicate balancing act – promoting regional autonomy and specialization while ensuring that these regional entities do not become insular or disruptive to global unity and cooperation.

Functional Organizations:

Current Examples: The United Nations system includes various specialized agencies like the World Health Organization (WHO) for health-related issues and the World Trade Organization (WTO) for trade matters. These organizations are focused on specific sectors, drawing expertise from around the world to address targeted concerns.

Advantages: The primary advantage of these functional organizations is their deep specialization. With a concentrated focus on particular sectors, these bodies can accumulate vast expertise, enabling them to develop innovative solutions and react quickly to challenges within their purview. This specialization also allows for a more streamlined approach, free from the broader political considerations that often bog down larger organizations like the UN. Furthermore, these organizations can serve as valuable forums for international collaboration, bringing together experts and stakeholders from various countries to work on common goals.

Potential Challenges: Despite their advantages, functional organizations are not without their issues. One significant challenge is the potential for overlapping responsibilities and jurisdictions, particularly in areas where the mandates of different organizations intersect. This overlap can lead to inefficiency, confusion, and sometimes even conflict over which organization has the lead on particular issues. Additionally, the effectiveness of these organizations depends heavily on their leadership and governance structures. There is a risk that these entities could become overly influenced by certain member states or external actors, skewing their priorities and undermining their impartiality. This could result in a scenario where these specialized bodies, instead of acting as neutral arbiters or facilitators, become tools for advancing specific national or corporate interests.

Navigating the Challenges: To maximize the benefits and minimize the risks associated with functional organizations, there must be clear, transparent, and fair governance structures in place. This includes ensuring diverse and equitable representation in decision-making processes and establishing robust mechanisms for coordination and conflict resolution between different organizations. Furthermore, maintaining a balance between specialization and broader policy coherence is essential. These organizations should not operate in isolation but rather as part of a coordinated global system that aligns their specialized efforts with the broader goals of international peace, development, and human rights.

Direct Diplomacy:

Historical Precedence: The landscape of international relations has been historically shaped through direct diplomacy, long before the advent of global organizations like the United Nations. The use of treaties, accords, and direct negotiations has been the traditional mechanism for managing international affairs, with many of the world's historical milestones being the result of such direct interactions between states.

Advantages: Direct diplomacy offers several compelling advantages. It fosters a more immediate and potentially more honest dialogue between nations, as there are no intermediaries to dilute or reinterpret the messages. This directness can lead to more tailored and specific agreements, closely aligned with the interests and needs of the negotiating parties. Nations engaged in direct diplomacy are often more invested in the outcomes, as they have a direct hand in shaping the agreements. This can result in a stronger commitment to implementing and adhering to the terms of these agreements, as they are not seen as externally imposed but rather as mutually agreed upon.

Potential Challenges: However, direct diplomacy is not without its significant challenges. One of the most glaring issues is the potential for power imbalances. In negotiations between a very powerful nation and a much weaker one, there is a risk that the outcomes will favor the stronger party, potentially leading to exploitative or unfair agreements. Furthermore, the absence of a neutral mediator can make it difficult to reach a consensus, particularly in highly contentious issues. Another major challenge is the lack of a centralized mechanism to monitor and enforce compliance with the agreements reached through direct diplomacy. Without this oversight, there is a risk that nations might not adhere to their commitments, leading to instability and mistrust in international relations.

Mitigating the Risks: To address these challenges, there needs to be a concerted effort to create frameworks or platforms that can facilitate more balanced and fair direct negotiations. This could involve the use of third-party mediators or the establishment of international norms and principles that guide bilateral or multilateral negotiations. Additionally, there could be mechanisms for smaller or weaker nations to band together to balance power dynamics in negotiations with larger states. Finally, the international community must find innovative ways to monitor and ensure compliance with agreements reached through direct diplomacy, perhaps through mutually agreed-upon verification measures or international oversight bodies.

In Conclusion

While the UN was founded with noble intentions, the concerns around its overreach and potential dominance cannot be ignored. As the world grapples with these concerns, it's essential to explore alternative structures that can preserve the essence of global cooperation while minimizing the risks associated with a singular dominant entity. Whether it's through regional alliances, functional organizations, or direct diplomacy, the goal remains the same: a collaborative world where nations work together for the collective good without fearing the overshadowing specter of a single overpowering entity.

Encouraging National Sovereignty While Promoting Global Cooperation

The balancing act between upholding national sovereignty and fostering global cooperation is one of the most intricate challenges facing the international community today. The emergence of the United Nations and its myriad of specialized agencies was seen as a beacon of hope post-World War II, aiming to ensure world peace and foster international collaboration. However, as with any potent entity, concerns surrounding its intentions and the fear of overreach become unavoidable. Here's a deeper dive into how we can strike a balance:

Respecting Local Context:

Historical Mistakes: The global community has often witnessed the pitfalls of implementing one-size-fits-all strategies. There are numerous historical examples where global initiatives have faltered due to a lack of understanding and respect for local contexts. Developmental policies, humanitarian interventions, and even peacekeeping missions have at times caused more harm than good, as they were applied uniformly without consideration of the unique cultural, economic, and political landscapes of different regions. Such mistakes highlight the importance of context in global policymaking.

Adaptive Frameworks: The future of effective global cooperation lies in the adoption of adaptive frameworks. These frameworks need to establish core universal principles that resonate with the common goals of humanity, such as peace, justice, and sustainability. However, they must also be flexible enough to allow for customization according to local needs and contexts. This adaptability will enable global goals to be pursued in a manner that is sensitive to and synergistic with local conditions, thereby enhancing the likelihood of success and acceptance.

Localized Implementation: A key component of making global policies work is the engagement with and empowerment of local stakeholders. This means not just consulting with national governments, but also involving local NGOs, community leaders, and civil society groups in the implementation process. By doing so, global initiatives can benefit from on-the-ground insights and expertise, ensuring that their implementation is not only contextually relevant but also inclusive and participatory. Such an approach fosters a sense of ownership among local populations, which is critical for the long-term sustainability and effectiveness of any global initiative.

Feedback Mechanisms and Course Correction: To truly respect local contexts, global bodies must establish robust feedback mechanisms that allow for continuous monitoring and evaluation of their initiatives. This includes being open to criticism and willing to make necessary adjustments when strategies are not working as intended. Such a dynamic approach, which embraces learning and evolution based on real-world experiences and outcomes, is crucial in ensuring that global cooperation does not become a rigid imposition of ideas but remains a fluid and responsive process that genuinely serves the needs of all stakeholders involved.

Training and Capacity Building: Respecting local context also involves building the capacity of local institutions and individuals so that they can effectively participate in and contribute to global initiatives. This can be achieved through training programs, knowledge exchange initiatives, and the provision of technical and financial resources. By strengthening local capabilities, the global community not only respects but also enhances the agency of local actors, making them equal partners in the pursuit of shared global objectives.

Empowering Local Governance:

Grassroots Movements:

- **Critical Role in Societal Transformation:** Grassroots movements have historically been the cradle of societal transformation. By nurturing these movements, global entities like the UN can tap into a reservoir of local knowledge and passion. These movements possess an intimate understanding of their community's needs, struggles, and aspirations, making them invaluable allies in addressing local issues.

- **Facilitating Autonomy:** The empowerment of grassroots movements will shift decision-making closer to those affected by these decisions. This shift would ensure that policies are not just parachuted in from afar but are born from the very soil they are meant to nourish. Such bottom-up approaches are essential in preserving the cultural, social, and political integrity of local communities.

Capacity Building:

- **A Shift from Solution Imposition to Facilitation:** The focus needs to shift from imposing one-size-fits-all solutions to facilitating local problem-solving capabilities. This involves investing in local institutions, enhancing their operational capacities, and providing them with the tools and resources necessary to tackle their unique challenges.

- **Sustainable Development Through Empowerment:** By empowering local entities, the UN would be planting seeds for sustainable development that are more likely to bear fruit as they are rooted in the local context. This empowerment is not just about providing resources but also about respecting and harnessing local knowledge and practices.

The Role of Technology:

- **Bridging Gaps and Fostering Collaboration:** In the age of globalization, technology can bridge vast distances, bringing together a tapestry of ideas and experiences. It can enable local governance bodies to collaborate with their global counterparts, share insights, and learn from each other's successes and failures.

- **Enhancing Efficiency and Participation:** Tools like mobile applications, online platforms, and digital forums can revolutionize how local governance functions. They can make processes more efficient, transparent, and inclusive, allowing for greater participation from the community. These technologies can also aid in gathering data, monitoring progress, and adapting strategies in real-time, making local governance more responsive to the changing needs of the community.

- **Overcoming Barriers:** Technology can play a crucial role in overcoming geographical, linguistic, and cultural barriers. It can democratize access to information, education, and resources, leveling the playing field for local entities that might otherwise be marginalized in the global discourse.

By focusing on empowering local governance, the UN can ensure that its initiatives are more than just top-down directives. Instead, they become catalysts for genuine, ground-up change that resonates with the people they are meant to serve. This approach would not only be more effective but also more in tune with the principles of self-determination and sovereignty that are the bedrock of a truly cooperative global community.

Inclusive Decision-making:

Bridging the Power Gap:

- **Restructuring for Fair Representation:** The United Nations, particularly the Security Council, must undergo structural changes to rectify the current power imbalances. This would involve redefining the veto power to prevent its misuse by the permanent members and ensuring fairer representation of all member nations, regardless of their economic or military might. Such a restructuring will require the major powers to cede some of their control, a necessary step for a more democratic global governance system.

- **Leveling the Playing Field:** The aim is to create a level playing field where smaller or less influential countries have an equal say in shaping global policies. This change will not only enhance the legitimacy of the UN but will also prevent it from being perceived as a tool for advancing the interests of a few powerful nations.

Platform for Dialogue:

- **Open Forums for All Nations:** Establishing open forums where every nation, regardless of size or power, can express their opinions and concerns is essential. These forums should facilitate genuine dialogue and exchange of ideas, leading to policies that reflect the collective will rather than the dictates of a few.

- **Cultivating a Collaborative Environment:** The focus should be on fostering an environment where nations feel encouraged to contribute, debate, and collaborate. This inclusive approach will likely lead to more innovative and effective solutions to global challenges, as it draws on a wider pool of experiences and viewpoints.

Feedback Mechanisms:

- **Dynamic Policy Adaptation:** Implementing robust feedback mechanisms is crucial for ensuring that policies remain relevant and effective. These mechanisms would allow for the continuous assessment of global initiatives, with the flexibility to adapt and modify them based on real-time feedback from the nations involved.

- **Empowering Nations through Feedback:** By allowing nations to provide feedback on the impact of policies, the UN would enable them to play an active role in the policy-making process. This approach ensures that global strategies are grounded in reality and responsive to the diverse needs of member nations.

- **Accountability and Transparency:** These feedback systems would also serve as tools for accountability, ensuring that the UN's actions are transparent and aligned with its stated objectives. It would also allow member states and the global community to hold the UN accountable for its decisions and their outcomes.

In conclusion, inclusive decision-making is not just about giving every nation a seat at the table; it's about genuinely considering and incorporating their inputs into global policies. This approach would not only democratize the UN's operations but also enhance its effectiveness and credibility. By ensuring that all voices are heard and valued, the UN can transform into a truly representative and responsive global body, effectively balancing national sovereignty with the need for global cooperation.

The fear that global bodies, like the United Nations, might prioritize global directives at the expense of national sovereignty is valid. However, the international community's challenge is to evolve a system where nations don't feel subjugated but empowered, where global cooperation doesn't overshadow but amplifies national identities. Achieving this delicate balance will be pivotal in shaping a harmonious global future.

In conclusion, while the need for global cooperation is undeniable, it is paramount to ensure that this doesn't erode the unique identities and sovereignties of individual nations. Whether through reforms within the UN or by exploring alternative models of collaboration, the world must move towards a system where every nation feels represented, valued, and in control of its destiny, free from overarching control or a dystopian narrative.

Chapter 13
Grassroots Movements and Public Influence

Role of Civil Society and NGOs in Counterbalancing the U.N.'s Alleged Ambitions

Civil society, including local communities, activists, and honest non-governmental organizations (NGOs), holds a unique power in the global landscape. Acting as a voice for the voiceless and providing localized solutions, these entities often counterbalance the sweeping and sometimes impersonal policies of larger organizations like the United Nations. When the global narrative seems to be veering towards monopolistic control, it's these grassroots institutions that often stand in defense of local needs and rights.

Counter-narrative to UN Directives:

Depth Over Breadth:

- **Focused Solutions:** Grassroots organizations and NGOs, with their deep-rooted presence in communities, are uniquely positioned to provide more focused and tailored solutions to local problems. Their intimate understanding of local needs allows them to craft initiatives that are more effective and relevant than the U.N.'s broader, one-size-fits-all approach.

- **Challenging Top-Down Policies:** These organizations often serve as critical checks to the U.N.'s top-down policies. By bringing attention to the gaps and flaws in these policies, they can force reconsiderations and modifications that better align with on-the-ground realities.

- **Voices of the Marginalized:** Non-corrupt NGOs and civil society groups are pivotal in raising the voices of marginalized communities that might be overlooked or underrepresented in the U.N.'s global agenda. By highlighting these voices, they ensure that global initiatives are more inclusive and just.

Cultural Sensitivity:

- **Preserving Local Traditions:** Non-corrupt NGOs are acutely aware of the importance of preserving cultural heritage and traditions. Their efforts often focus on integrating these aspects into developmental or humanitarian initiatives, thus countering the U.N.'s tendency to overlook these crucial elements.

- **Advocates for Cultural Identity:** In their role as defenders of local cultures, these organizations actively advocate for the importance of cultural identity in the face of globalization. They work to ensure that development does not equate to cultural homogenization.

- **Educating Global Entities:** Through their work, grassroots movements and Non-corrupt NGOs also educate larger entities like the U.N. about the significance of cultural nuances. Their insights can lead to more sensitive and effective policies that respect and honor local traditions and practices.

While the U.N. and similar entities aim for global solutions, it is often the work of local NGOs and civil society that provides the necessary balance, ensuring that policies are not only globally relevant but also locally applicable and respectful of cultural diversity. Their role in creating a counter-narrative to U.N. directives is crucial, not just for the success of these policies, but for the preservation of local identities and traditions in an increasingly globalized world. The grassroots approach of these organizations will continue to be vital in ensuring that global ambitions do not override local realities and needs.

Watchdogs of the U.N.:

Auditing Power:

- **Rigorous Scrutiny:** These civil society organizations function as vigilant auditors of the U.N.'s operations. They meticulously examine policies, initiatives, and spending, ensuring that every action taken is transparent and aligns with the organization's stated objectives and global ethical standards.

- **Exposing Discrepancies:** By rigorously scrutinizing the U.N.'s activities, these groups are often the first to spot and expose any discrepancies or deviations from the U.N.'s own guidelines and missions. Their findings frequently lead to public pressure for reform and correction within the U.N. system.

- **Guardians of Integrity:** The persistent vigilance of these organizations is vital in maintaining the integrity of the U.N. They serve as guardians, ensuring that the organization remains true to its principles of global welfare and does not deviate towards self-serving agendas.

Whistleblowing:

- **Exposing Internal Issues:** There have been pivotal moments where whistleblowers, often supported and protected by non-corrupt NGOs, have come forward with critical information about mismanagement or unethical practices within the U.N. These disclosures have been instrumental in bringing necessary reforms and accountability to the institution.

- **Empowering Insiders:** Non-corrupt NGOs not only facilitate whistleblowing but also empower insiders within the U.N. to speak up against wrongdoing. They provide legal, moral, and sometimes financial support, enabling these individuals to challenge the organization from within.

- **Public Awareness and Reform:** The act of whistleblowing, amplified by civil society groups, plays a crucial role in raising public awareness about the U.N.'s failings. It often acts as a catalyst for internal reform, pushing the organization to address its shortcomings and adhere more closely to its foundational values of transparency and accountability.

The role of civil society organizations and non-corrupt NGOs as watchdogs of the United Nations is an essential component in the global checks and balances system. Their activities in auditing the U.N.'s actions and supporting whistleblowers not only foster transparency and accountability but also ensure that the U.N. remains a servant to global needs rather than a master of global dictates. Their continuous vigilance is a powerful counterforce to any potential overreach or deviation from the U.N.'s core principles and missions.

Advocacy and Lobbying:

Mass Mobilization:

- **Grassroots Campaigns:** Civil societies and non-corrupt NGOs are adept at organizing grassroots campaigns, turning local concerns into global issues. These campaigns often involve community rallies, educational seminars, and widespread online movements that galvanize public opinion.

- **Public Sentiment as a Force:** The ability to stir and harness public sentiment is one of these entities' most potent tools. They can transform public outrage into a formidable force that challenges the U.N.'s actions and policies, demanding transparency and accountability.

- **Empowering Voices:** By mobilizing the masses, these groups empower individual voices, creating a collective roar that is hard for global entities like the U.N. to ignore. This mass mobilization can lead to significant policy shifts and reforms within the U.N., driven by the sheer force of public demand.

International Pressure:

- **Global Advocacy Networks:** NGOs work in a networked manner, often forming alliances across borders. By doing so, they amplify their voice and extend their reach, creating a ripple effect of advocacy and lobbying that transcends national boundaries.

- **Influencing Global Agendas:** With coordinated effort, non-corrupt NGOs can bring specific issues to the forefront of global discussions. They can influence international forums, conferences, and even U.N. assemblies, ensuring that issues ignored or downplayed by the U.N. find a global audience.

- **Diplomatic Leverage:** These organizations often engage in diplomatic lobbying, using their influence to sway international opinion and, in some cases, even governmental policies. This international pressure can force the U.N. to reconsider its strategies and approaches, especially if they are seen as detrimental to the broader global community.

The role of civil society and NGOs in advocacy and lobbying forms a critical part of the checks and balances against the United Nations' power. Through mass mobilization and international pressure, these entities have the capability to reshape narratives, influence policies, and ensure that the U.N. remains accountable to the people it serves. Their actions serve as a reminder that true power lies not in the hands of a few global elites, but in the united voice of the global citizenry, vigilant and ready to defend their rights and needs.

Alternative Aid and Development Channels:

Diverse Funding Sources:

- **Independent Financial Streams:** Non-corrupt NGOs often tap into a variety of funding sources, including private donations, crowdfunding, and grants from independent foundations. This diversified financial portfolio enables them to maintain autonomy, free from the strings that often accompany U.N.-sourced funding.

- **Resisting Homogenization:** By not relying solely on U.N. funds, these organizations can resist the homogenizing effect of large-scale global aid. This independence is crucial in promoting alternative viewpoints and methodologies in development work.

- **Agility and Responsiveness:** The variety in funding also allows non-corrupt NGOs to be more agile and responsive. They can mobilize resources quickly and are not bogged down by the often cumbersome bureaucratic processes that can plague U.N.-sponsored projects.

Localized Solutions:

- **Community-Centric Approaches:** Non-corrupt NGOs, particularly those working at the grassroots level, excel in developing community-centric solutions. They work closely with local populations to understand their specific needs and challenges, leading to more effective and sustainable outcomes.

- **Adaptive Strategies:** Unlike the blanket approaches that may be favored by the U.N., NGOs are adept at adapting their strategies to fit the unique socio-cultural and economic contexts of each community they serve. This flexibility ensures that solutions are not just imposed but are grown organically within the community.

- **Empowerment over Dependency:** A key focus of these alternative aid channels is to empower communities rather than create dependency. They aim to build local capacities, ensuring that communities are equipped to address their challenges independently in the long run.

In summary, alternative aid and development channels offered by civil society and non-corrupt NGOs present a vital counterforce to the U.N.'s alleged ambitions for global dominance. Their diverse funding sources ensure independence and agility, while their localized, community-centric solutions provide effective and sustainable outcomes. By prioritizing empowerment over dependency, these organizations champion a more equitable and diverse approach to global development, standing in stark contrast to the one-size-fits-all solutions that critics accuse the U.N. of promoting. This decentralized approach to aid and development not only challenges the U.N.'s narrative but also underscores the importance of diverse perspectives and methodologies in addressing global challenges.

Conclusion:

While the U.N., with its vast resources and global reach, stands as a colossus in the international arena, the agile, localized, and focused efforts of civil societies and non-corrupt NGOs provide a necessary counterbalance. Their commitment to ground-level realities and the ability to mobilize public sentiment act as potent checks against any entity's drive towards unwarranted dominance. Through their efforts, the narrative of global cooperation remains democratic, ensuring that the voices of communities worldwide are not just heard, but resonate powerfully in the corridors of global decision-making.

Public Influence on International Policies: Challenging the Alleged Dominance of the U.N. and Its Allies

In an era marked by instant communication and vast digital networks, the voice of the masses is more potent than ever. However, as platforms grow, so does the boldness of international organizations like the U.N. and the World Economic Forum (WEF), as they're perceived to become more impervious to public sentiment. But history and modern mechanisms show the indomitable spirit of the public to influence policies, even those on the global stage.

Public Outcry and Protest:

Power of Physical Presence:

- **Unignorable Demonstrations:** The physical presence of protesters en masse in public spaces has a unique and powerful impact. These demonstrations, often covered extensively by media, send a clear and direct message to global bodies like the U.N. and WEF. They showcase the public's ability to physically manifest their dissent, making it impossible for these entities to ignore or downplay the issues raised.

- **Symbolic Landmarks:** Protests often occur at symbolic locations such as embassies, U.N. headquarters, or major international meetings. The choice of these sites is strategic, intended to draw attention to the specific actions or policies of these global entities, thus spotlighting the public's discontent with their perceived dominance.

Global Synergy:

- **Transnational Solidarity:** The global nature of modern protests is significant. Issues in one country can quickly gain international attention, leading to a domino effect of solidarity protests around the world. This transnational synergy demonstrates the global community's collective power against perceived injustices or overreach by international organizations.

- **Digital Amplification:** Social media and digital platforms play a critical role in amplifying these movements. They allow for rapid dissemination of information, mobilization of support, and coordination of actions across borders. This digital network turns local protests into global movements, creating a unified front that challenges the decisions and policies of international entities like the U.N. and WEF.

- **Influencing Policy Change:** These global protests, fueled by grassroots energy and digital mobilization, have the power to influence international policies. Public outcry and demonstrations can lead to policy reversals, amendments to international treaties, and even changes in the leadership of these organizations. They serve as a testament to the public's ability to hold these bodies accountable and challenge their perceived push for dominance.

Public outcry and protest remain potent tools for challenging the actions of international organizations like the U.N. and WEF. Through physical demonstrations, symbolic protests, and global digital networks, the public voice can resonate on the international stage, influencing policies and challenging the alleged dominance of these entities. The combined power of physical presence and global synergy, amplified by digital platforms, underscores the enduring strength of public influence in shaping global affairs.

Digital Campaigns and Movements:

Viral Momentum:

- **Unprecedented Reach and Speed:** The power of digital campaigns lies in their ability to achieve viral momentum almost instantaneously. Campaigns like #ClimateStrike or #BlackLivesMatter have demonstrated how quickly a message can spread across the globe, garnering millions of interactions, shares, and expressions of solidarity. This rapid diffusion of messages challenges the traditional speed and reach of international organizations like the U.N. and WEF.

- **Spurring Global Action:** These viral movements often transcend mere online activity, spurring real-world action. They lead to global marches, strikes, and demonstrations, significantly increasing public awareness and pressure on international policy matters. This shift from digital engagement to physical activism represents a new dynamic in global advocacy, where the line between online and offline influence becomes increasingly blurred.

Global Solidarity:

- **Unified Voice Across Borders:** Social media platforms have the unique ability to unite people from various countries and cultures around a single cause. They effectively break down geographic and cultural barriers, creating a sense of global community and solidarity. This collective voice is particularly powerful in challenging international policies and directives that are perceived as overreaching or detrimental to certain groups or regions.

- **Amplifying Marginalized Voices:** Digital platforms also play a crucial role in amplifying voices that might otherwise be marginalized or overlooked in traditional media. They provide an avenue for diverse perspectives to be heard, especially those from regions or groups that may not have direct representation in international forums like the U.N. or WEF.

- **Influencing Policy and Perception:** The ability of these digital movements to shape public perception and influence policy cannot be understated. They have forced international bodies to take notice, address public concerns, and in some cases, rethink their strategies or policies. The global solidarity fostered by these movements sends a clear message to these organizations: the public is watching, engaged, and ready to hold them accountable.

Digital campaigns and movements represent a significant shift in how the public can influence international policies and challenge the perceived dominance of entities like the U.N. and WEF. Through viral momentum and global solidarity, these digital platforms empower individuals worldwide to unite, voice their concerns, and effect change, proving that the spirit of the public remains a formidable force in shaping the global narrative.

Petitions and Collective Bargaining:

Power in Numbers:

- **Unyielding Influence:** The advent of online petitions marks a paradigm shift in how the public engages with and influences international policy. By gathering millions of signatures from around the world, these petitions convert individual concerns into a formidable collective demand. This aggregation of voices magnifies their impact, transforming them into a powerful tool for social and political change. It becomes increasingly challenging for global organizations like the U.N. and WEF to ignore these voices without risking public backlash.

- **A Tool for Accountability:** These petitions serve as a direct line of communication from the public to international decision-makers. The sheer volume of signatories sends a clear message that the public is not only observant but also willing to mobilize en masse. This collective action places additional pressure on these organizations to be transparent and accountable in their decision-making processes, ensuring that they remain aligned with the public's expectations and demands.

Highlighting Underrepresented Issues:

- **Bringing Neglected Topics to Light:** Online petitions have the unique capacity to spotlight issues that may not receive attention in mainstream discussions or agendas set by major global entities. They serve as a platform for raising awareness about underrepresented or marginalized concerns, ensuring a broader and more inclusive discourse on international matters.

- **Global Reach and Representation:** The global reach of these petitions ensures that voices from all corners of the world are heard, including those from regions or communities that may not have a strong presence or representation in global forums. By highlighting these diverse perspectives, petitions challenge the alleged homogeneity of the U.N.'s agenda and push for a more multifaceted approach to global governance.

- **Direct Impact on Policy:** The effectiveness of these petitions is not merely symbolic. They have led to tangible changes in policies and practices of international bodies. By raising awareness and mobilizing public opinion, petitions can sway policymakers, leading to revisions, amendments, or even the abandonment of certain policies that do not align with the collective will of the global community.

Petitions and collective bargaining serve as potent tools in the public's arsenal to challenge the perceived dominance of entities like the U.N. and the WEF. By leveraging the power of numbers and highlighting underrepresented issues, they not only ensure that a broader spectrum of voices is heard but also hold these organizations accountable to the global populace they claim to serve. This dynamic interaction between grassroots activism and international policymaking underscores the evolving nature of global governance in the digital age.

Promotion of Alternative Narratives:

Diverse Voices:

- **Echo Chamber Disruption:** In a landscape often dominated by mainstream media narratives, alternative platforms like blogs, podcasts, and independent news sites emerge as crucial spaces for dissent and discussion. These platforms dismantle the echo chambers created by traditional media, providing a haven for diverse, often marginalized voices. They allow narratives that challenge or oppose the U.N.'s directives to gain traction and spark public discourse.

- **Cultivating Critical Thinking:** By offering a spectrum of opinions and analyses, these alternative media sources encourage the audience to engage in critical thinking. They counter the perceived homogenization of perspectives fostered by mainstream media, ensuring that public opinion is not unidirectionally shaped by a single narrative. This diversity of viewpoints is essential in a world where international policies can have far-reaching and varied impacts on different communities and regions.

Exposés and Deep-dives:

- **Illuminating the Obscure:** Independent content creators often venture where mainstream media might tread cautiously. They undertake comprehensive deep-dives into the complex world of international policies, agreements, and the inner workings of entities like the U.N. and WEF. Their detailed exposés illuminate aspects that are often shrouded in complexity, making them accessible and understandable to the general public.

- **Uncovering Hidden Agendas:** These deep-dives frequently reveal aspects of policies or decisions that might have otherwise remained obscured. They expose the intricacies and potential hidden agendas behind seemingly benign initiatives, prompting public scrutiny and debate. By dissecting and questioning the actions of global organizations, they ensure that these entities remain under the watchful eye of an informed public.

- **Triggering Accountability:** The revelations and insights provided by these alternative narratives can trigger significant public outcry, leading to demands for accountability and transparency from international organizations. They play a pivotal role in ensuring that the actions of the U.N. and its allies are not just accepted at face value but are critically evaluated and scrutinized.

In essence, the promotion of alternative narratives through diverse voices and in-depth analyses plays a critical role in countering the alleged dominance of the U.N. and its allies. It ensures that the global public remains informed, engaged, and critical of the decisions that shape their world. This dynamic ecosystem of information and opinion forms a vital part of the checks and balances necessary in a world where international cooperation and governance are more interconnected than ever.

Election of Sovereignty-focused Leaders:

A Democratic Check:

- **Empowerment Through Voting:** The democratic process empowers citizens to shape their governance and international stance. Electing leaders committed to safeguarding national sovereignty acts as a critical counterbalance to the perceived encroaching power of international bodies like the U.N. and the WEF. When the electorate prioritizes sovereignty, it sends a clear message to these global organizations about the limits of their influence.

- **Manifesting Public Will:** The election of such leaders is not merely a political act but a manifestation of the public's will. It reflects a collective stance that values self-determination over global directives that might not align with national interests. By making informed choices at the polls, citizens assert their role in determining how their nation interacts with and responds to international organizations.

Re-negotiating Global Position:

- **Strategic Review of Alliances:** Leaders who emphasize sovereignty will likely undertake a strategic review of their nation's international alliances and commitments. This can lead to a re-negotiation of terms in international treaties or a recalibration of their role in global organizations to better serve national interests.

- **Balancing Global and National Interests:** These leaders will strive to strike a balance between participating in global cooperation and preserving the unique needs and aspirations of their nation. They act as gatekeepers, ensuring that international engagements are beneficial and do not compromise the country's autonomy or values.

- **Setting Precedents for Others:** The actions of these leaders can set precedents, encouraging other nations to follow suit. This could lead to a ripple effect, where more countries start asserting their sovereignty, potentially reshaping the global order to be more respectful of individual nation-states' rights and preferences.

Global Implications:

- **Shifting Power Dynamics:** The election of sovereignty-focused leaders can significantly shift the power dynamics between nations and global entities. It emphasizes that while international cooperation is vital, it should not override the fundamental rights and decisions of sovereign states.

- **Reinforcing the Principle of Equality:** Such leadership reinforces the principle that all nations, regardless of size or power, have an equal stake in global affairs. It ensures that international cooperation is based on mutual respect and fairness rather than perceived dominance by a few powerful entities.

The election of leaders who prioritize national sovereignty serves as a democratic check against the perceived overreach of international organizations. It represents the public's desire for governance that respects national uniqueness while engaging constructively on the global stage. This approach not only strengthens the autonomy of individual nations but also contributes to a more balanced and equitable global order.

The might of international bodies like the U.N. and the WEF, while formidable, is consistently balanced by the collective voice of the global populace. Through both tangible actions and digital movements, the masses ensure that these organizations remain, at their core, accountable to the very people they represent. The era of digital activism has empowered individuals like never before, ensuring that global cooperation doesn't trample individual rights and national sovereignty.

Chapter 14
Conclusion

Recap of Main Arguments

The United Nations: A symbol of hope, or an emblem of overreach? As we delve into the multifaceted role and influence of the UN, it's essential to critically assess its trajectory and intentions.

1. History and Formation: Overreach Beyond Original Mandate

Born from the ashes of World War II, the United Nations was initially hailed as humanity's last hope to avert global conflicts of such magnitude. Yet, as decades unfolded, the UN's role expanded significantly, far beyond its original remit of preventing large-scale wars. This expansion into various domains, many of which intrude upon the sovereignty of nations, raises critical alarms. It compels us to scrutinize whether the UN is overreaching beyond its foundational charter. Questions loom large: Are the actions of the UN genuinely aimed at the collective welfare of the global populace, or do they mask a more ambitious goal of global domination? The trajectory of the UN from a mere peacekeeping entity to one that seemingly seeks to influence and direct national policies across diverse spectrums points towards a concerning shift. This shift, many argue, signals not just a deviation from its original purpose but a deliberate stride towards establishing a centralized global authority. Such moves, often wrapped in the cloak of benevolence, potentially serve ulterior motives that align with the interests of a select group of global elites, rather than the diverse needs of the world's nations.

2. Structural Disparities: The Security Council's Dominance and Democratic Deficit

The structural composition of the United Nations, especially the Security Council, stands as a glaring symbol of unequal power dynamics. The privilege of the veto power, held by a mere handful of nations, blatantly contradicts the principles of democratic equity and fair representation. This concentration of authority in the hands of a few not only undermines the legitimacy of the UN as a truly global entity but also paves the way for these dominant nations to orchestrate and manipulate international policies. The result is a skewed system where global decisions are disproportionately influenced by the interests and strategies of these select countries. It effectively silences the voices of smaller, less powerful nations, whose concerns and needs are often overshadowed or outright ignored. This imbalance fosters a breeding ground for the major powers to impose their will on the international stage, shaping the UN's actions to align with their national interests rather than the collective good. Such a dynamic casts a long shadow over the UN's claim to be an impartial and equitable forum for global governance, raising questions about its true role: is it a facilitator of global cooperation or a tool for the perpetuation of the status quo in global power hierarchies?

3. Economic and Financial Grip: The UN's Overarching Influence Over Global Economies

The United Nations, through its affiliates like the International Monetary Fund (IMF) and World Bank, exerts a considerable influence on the global financial landscape. This dominant position enables the UN to steer the economic policies of nations, especially those dependent on financial aid. The imposition of sanctions serves as a testament to this power, often bending nations to the will of a global agenda set by the more influential members of the UN. The consequences of such an economic grip are profound and multi-faceted. Nations find themselves entangled in a web of financial dependence, their sovereignty undermined by the need to align with policies and directives that may run counter to their local needs and priorities. This financial might is not just a tool for economic management but becomes an instrument of geopolitical strategy, where aid and sanctions are used selectively to reward compliance and punish dissent. The narrative that emerges is one of control – financial strings are pulled to choreograph a dance of nations, all moving to the tune set by the UN and its dominant member states. This global financial orchestration, while wrapped in the guise of economic stability and development, often masks a more insidious motive of maintaining and expanding influence over sovereign nations.

4. Digitalization Drive: The Double-Edged Sword of the UN's Technological Agenda

The United Nations' aggressive push towards digitalization and its adoption of technology-driven solutions ostensibly aims to modernize and streamline global systems. However, this march towards a digital future raises critical concerns about privacy, autonomy, and surveillance. The shift towards Central Bank Digital Currencies (CBDCs), Digital IDs, and smart city infrastructures, while portrayed as steps towards inclusivity and efficiency, simultaneously pave the way for unprecedented levels of monitoring and data collection. This digital leap, under the auspices of the UN, risks evolving into a tool for pervasive surveillance, where the minutiae of individual lives are no longer private but are elements in a vast, analyzable dataset.

The implications of such an environment extend far beyond convenience and efficiency. The very essence of personal freedom and privacy is at stake. With every transaction, movement, and interaction potentially tracked and scrutinized, the notion of a free society becomes questionable. Digital IDs, lauded for their ability to streamline services, also possess the potential to function as instruments of social and political control. The power to switch off an individual's digital identity could equate to denying them access to fundamental services and rights.

The UN's role in advocating for these digital frameworks, therefore, is viewed by some as more than a mere facilitation of global modernization. It is perceived as a strategic move towards establishing a global infrastructure that can monitor, influence, and control the populace under the guise of technological advancement. This digital dominion, while veiled in the language of progress and innovation, might be the cornerstone of a new world order where individual liberties are subservient to the watchful eye of a technocratic elite.

5.   The SDG Plan: A Cloak for Uniformity and Control?

The United Nations' Sustainable Development Goals (SDGs) are often lauded as a roadmap towards a more sustainable and equitable future. However, a critical examination reveals a different narrative. These goals, while ostensibly aiming to address global challenges such as poverty, hunger, and climate change, are increasingly viewed by skeptics as instruments of imposing a one-size-fits-all development model across diverse nations. This approach not only overlooks the unique socio-economic and cultural contexts of different regions but also raises questions about the loss of national autonomy in setting development agendas.

Far from being mere guidelines, the SDGs are often tied to financial incentives and aid, effectively pressuring nations to align with a set of standards that may not suit their specific needs or respect their cultural heritage. This has been likened to a new form of neo-colonialism, where compliance with these global goals becomes a prerequisite for financial support, leaving little room for independent or alternative development paths. The irony of the situation becomes stark when considering the economic outcomes for companies that have attempted to implement these goals. Far from profiting, most companies find themselves at a financial loss, raising the question of whether these goals are truly designed for the betterment of societies or if they serve as a covert mechanism for economic and political influence by global elites.

Furthermore, the implementation of the SDGs often favors multinational corporations and global institutions, which have the resources and reach to influence these goals' trajectory. This creates a scenario where local businesses and communities are marginalized, and their voices go unheard in the global development discourse. The SDGs, thus, can be seen as a strategic tool for perpetuating a global hierarchy where the priorities and interests of powerful entities are advanced under the guise of sustainable development, often at the expense of genuine local empowerment and autonomy.

6. Associations with Other International Entities: A Convergence of Elites?

The United Nations' alliances with various international entities, such as the World Economic Forum (WEF), have sparked intense debate and speculation about the real intentions behind these partnerships. On the surface, these collaborations are portrayed as concerted efforts towards global progress and sustainable development. However, a more critical perspective suggests a darker narrative, where these connections represent a confluence of powerful, elite entities orchestrating global policies and agendas.

The concern is that these coalitions are less about altruistic global advancement and more about consolidating power and influence in the hands of a few. This perspective posits that the UN, in partnership with organizations like the WEF, is not just facilitating international cooperation but is actively participating in shaping a future that aligns with the interests of the global elite. This perceived alignment raises questions about whose interests are truly being served — those of the broader global community or a select group of influential players?

Such associations are seen as mechanisms for the global elite to maintain and expand their influence, often at the expense of democratic processes and the sovereignty of individual nations. The fear is that these partnerships could lead to a scenario where global policies and initiatives, instead of being the product of a diverse and representative decision-making process, are dictated by a small group of powerful individuals and organizations. This could result in a world where the priorities and concerns of the general population are secondary to the ambitions and objectives of a global ruling class.

7. National Sovereignty vs. Global Cooperation: A Delicate Balancing Act or an Overbearing Influence?

In the quest for a harmonious global community, the United Nations often finds itself at the epicenter of a contentious debate: the trade-off between national sovereignty and global cooperation. This ongoing struggle encapsulates one of the primary critiques against the UN, which is the perceived encroachment on national autonomy in favor of a universalized agenda.

Proponents of sovereignty argue that the UN's initiatives, while perhaps "well-intentioned", can impose constraints on individual nations' freedom to chart their own course. They view these global directives not as collaborative efforts but as tools for diluting national identity and self-determination. The critical concern here is whether the UN's role is overreaching, potentially leading to a diminished respect for the unique political, cultural, and social fabric of each member state.

This perspective posits that the UN's push for global cooperation might inadvertently (or deliberately, as many critics argue) suppress the distinctiveness of nations under the guise of universal standards and goals. The fear is that in the pursuit of a globalized agenda, the UN will not only overlook but actively override the specific needs, traditions, and aspirations of individual countries. This leads to growing apprehension about the UN's true intentions and the potential risks posed to national independence and identity in the face of an expanding global cooperative framework.

8. Grassroots Movements and Public Influence: The Indomitable Check Against Centralized Power

The undeniable power of grassroots movements and public influence stands as a bulwark against the perceived attempt by the United Nations and its partners to establish centralized control over global affairs. This power manifests through grassroots organizations and honest NGOs which work relentlessly on the ground, often untouched by corrupt influences and directly in touch with the local realities. They serve as the vanguard of the common people's interests, often standing in stark contrast to the expansive reach of the UN.

Similarly, global digital campaigns and movements harness the power of collective public sentiment, creating a digital wave that challenges and scrutinizes every move of the United Nations. These campaigns serve as a digital torchlight, exposing and dissecting the UN's actions, ensuring that any attempts at overreach do not go unnoticed or unchallenged.

This grassroots and public domain, therefore, emerges as a critical element in maintaining a balance of power. It represents a sphere where the voice of the average individual can still resonate and have an impact, providing a necessary check against the might of the UN and ensuring that its actions remain aligned with the true needs and wishes of the global populace. This dynamic interplay between the UN and the grassroots movements underscores the ongoing struggle and the critical role of public influence in shaping global policies and directives.

In wrapping up our critical examination, we confront a pivotal inquiry: Does the United Nations stand as a guardian of global peace and cooperation, or does it mask a more insidious ambition for global dominance? The evidence and analysis presented lean heavily towards the latter – a scenario where the UN, under the guise of benevolence, might be orchestrating a grander scheme of global control.

It is crucial, therefore, to maintain a vigilant and questioning stance. The complexities and intricacies of global politics demand that we scrutinize the actions and intentions of the United Nations and its partners with a discerning eye. We must be informed and proactive in our approach to ensure that the balance of power does not tip overwhelmingly in favor of any single entity, especially one with as much influence and reach as the UN.

The future we envisage for the coming generations must be rooted in true cooperation, mutual respect, and a genuine desire for shared prosperity. It should not be a future where the many are subjugated to the will of the few, cloaked under the banner of global unity and progress. As we close this chapter, let us remember that the responsibility to shape this future does not lie solely with global organizations but also with each one of us, as active and informed members of the global community.

A Look Towards the Future

As we peer into the future, it becomes evident that it is not a predetermined path but a complex fabric shaped by today's decisions and actions. In this intricate tapestry, the United Nations stands out as a formidable entity, casting a long shadow over global affairs. This prominence necessitates a rigorous and critical examination of the UN's expanding influence and the potential ramifications it holds for the future of our world.

The blend of conspiracy theories and legitimate apprehensions presents a multifaceted and often unsettling perspective of the direction in which the UN could steer global dynamics. The possibility of the organization wielding its power to shape a future that aligns more with its own vision than with the diverse aspirations of the global populace is a concern that cannot be ignored.

As we stand at this crossroads, the responsibility to remain alert and critically engaged falls on each of us. The future of our world – whether it will be dictated by a singular global authority or guided by the collective will of a genuinely cooperative international community – hinges on our awareness, understanding, and actions in the present.

1. The Expanding Dominance of the UN

In a world grappling with issues like climate change, health emergencies, and geopolitical upheavals, there's a discernible shift towards seeking globalized solutions. The United Nations, with its extensive network and influence over member nations, positions itself as the orchestrator of this global approach. Yet, this raises critical alarms when such a unifying perspective starts to overshadow and potentially override individual nation's priorities and agendas.

- Domination Over Diversity: While a globally centralized strategy promises efficiency, it inherently risks missing the intricate subtleties necessary to effectively address the unique challenges faced by different regions. There's a profound risk in embracing a universal policy model that could ultimately quash cultural uniqueness, erode national sovereignty, and undermine the autonomy of individual countries in managing their affairs.

- Threat to Personal Liberties: With the UN's power growing potentially unrestrained, there looms a scenario where global decrees and policies could start dictating personal life choices, infringing upon fundamental rights and freedoms. This overbearing influence of a global body may very well threaten the core principles of democracy and personal autonomy, leading to an era where individual preferences and liberties are compromised in favor of a homogenized global order.

2. Partnerships with Global Powerhouses:

The intricate relationships between the United Nations and other key global players, notably the World Economic Forum (WEF), are a source of growing concern and rampant speculation.

- Aligning of Global Visions: Questions arise over whether there exists a unified, secretive agenda pursued by these organizations. The apparent alignment of their objectives might suggest a deeper, possibly concealed collaboration aimed at sculpting the world to fit a specific vision. This alliance could, potentially, override the authentic needs and voices of nations and their citizens, favoring the ambitions of a select international elite.

- The Specter of a 'New World Order': Discussions about a 'New World Order' frequently emerge in this context, where the UN, along with other major global organizations, is perceived as central to the establishment of a singular, overpowering global governance structure. While such notions are often relegated to the realm of conspiracy theories, the increasing interconnections between the UN and these influential bodies do give impetus to these claims, suggesting an agenda for global dominance that transcends traditional national sovereignty and public choice.

3. The Digital Paradigm and Global Governance:

As we rapidly progress into the digital age, the integration of technology into the framework of global governance, particularly by entities like the United Nations, invites intense scrutiny and apprehension.

- The Rise of a Surveillance State: The digital revolution, under the guise of efficiency and global connectivity, harbors the risk of extensive surveillance. Initiatives championed by the UN, such as digital identification systems, Smart City projects, and the promotion of digital currencies, could be repurposed as instruments for incessant monitoring of citizens' activities, thereby eroding the fundamental right to privacy.

- Control of Data as a Control of Power: In our digital world, data is synonymous with power. If the UN, in partnership with global technology corporations, gains control over vast swathes of global data, the consequences will be far-reaching. This control could lead to the UN shaping global narratives, swaying political and social decisions, and potentially manipulating public perceptions on a massive scale. Such a concentration of data-driven power in the hands of an international organization like the UN raises alarms about a future where individual freedoms and national sovereignty are subjugated to a digital dominion governed from afar.

In confronting the immense and potentially alarming implications of the United Nations and its partners' increasing dominance, the onus falls upon global citizens to be ever-vigilant, well-informed, and actively engaged. The future, teetering on the brink of a UN-centric narrative, is not theirs alone to dictate. It is, in fact, a collective saga that must equally represent the diverse aspirations and voices of nations, communities, and individuals around the globe. As we step forward into an uncertain future, it is of paramount importance that this narrative upholds the principles of pluralism, democracy, and inclusivity. It should reflect the rich tapestry of our global family, resisting the gravitation towards a monolithic and potentially oppressive global order dictated by a single entity. Our collective vigilance and proactive engagement are the bulwarks against the overreaching ambitions of any international body, ensuring that the future we march towards is one of shared values, equitable opportunities, and respect for the sovereign identities that form our global community.

Ensuring a Balanced Future

In an era where global entities such as the United Nations hold substantial sway, the escalating worries about their potential for overarching dominance are not without merit. As we navigate towards the future, we are confronted with critical questions regarding the preservation of autonomy, identity, and sovereignty. It is imperative to ensure that this trajectory does not culminate in a homogenized global landscape, where the rich tapestry of diverse cultural, national, and individual identities is diminished or lost. This calls for a series of proactive measures and vigilant actions to safeguard against a one-dimensional world order. It necessitates a steadfast commitment to maintaining the delicate balance between global cooperation and the respect for distinct sovereignties, ensuring that the path forward is not just a unilateral narrative shaped by a select few but a pluralistic journey that truly reflects the multiplicity of the world's voices and perspectives.

1. **Staying Informed: The Bedrock of Resistance against Dominance**

    - **Deciphering Propaganda and Truth:** In an era saturated with information, the ability to distinguish between genuine facts and disguised propaganda is crucial. It is essential for individuals and nations alike to understand the underlying motives and agendas that drive international policies. This knowledge empowers them to make choices that align with their best interests, rather than being swayed by the dominating narratives of powerful global entities.

    - **Empowering Through Education:** A steadfast investment in education, especially focusing on global affairs, international relations, and media literacy, becomes imperative. Education is the key to fostering a populace that is not only informed but also capable of critically analyzing and questioning the global narratives put forth by entities like the United Nations. An educated global citizenry is less likely to succumb to the whims of a singular global agenda, ensuring a diverse and multi-perspective future.

2. **Championing Grassroots Movements: The Vanguard of Democratic Resilience**

   - **Empowerment through Ample Resources:** The essence of true democratic practice lies in grassroots movements. Despite often operating on shoestring budgets, these movements possess the intimate knowledge of local challenges and sentiments. By providing them with enhanced financial, logistical, and advocacy resources, we can bolster their capacity to implement solutions that resonate with local needs. This empowerment is a crucial step in ensuring that global agendas do not overshadow localized priorities.

   - **Fostering a Networked Resistance:** The creation of robust networks among grassroots organizations worldwide presents a formidable challenge to any form of centralized global control. Through collaboration and solidarity, these movements can share strategies, experiences, and resources, amplifying their impact. Such a network serves as a bulwark against the encroachment of global dominance, ensuring that diverse voices are not just heard but also shape the future in a meaningful way.

3. **Advocating for Unfettered Transparency: Building Trust through Openness**

   - **Embracing Open Source Governance:** To foster trust and dismantle suspicions, there is an urgent need to push for open source practices within international organizations. This move towards transparent governance would ensure that all policy discussions, decisions, and diplomatic negotiations are accessible to public scrutiny. This level of openness not only deters hidden agendas but also empowers the global community to engage actively in international discourse.

- **Rigorous Accountability Protocols:** Establishing robust accountability frameworks is critical for maintaining the integrity of international bodies like the UN. These protocols should be designed to closely monitor and evaluate the actions and outcomes of these bodies, ensuring they align with their stated objectives. With such mechanisms in place, any deviation or overreach can be swiftly identified, challenged, and corrected, ensuring these organizations truly serve the global populace.

4. **Embracing Participatory Governance: Fortifying Democracy from the Ground Up**

- **Catalyzing Active Voter Engagement:** In a world overshadowed by the looming influence of global organizations like the United Nations, fostering active voter participation becomes crucial. It's imperative to implement strategies that encourage a higher voter turnout, particularly targeting the youth, to ensure the elected leaders genuinely mirror the desires and aspirations of the populace. This active civic engagement can serve as a bulwark against the encroachment of global bodies on national sovereignty.

- **Advocating for Decentralized Power Structures:** The concentration of power within global entities like the UN raises profound questions about the future of democratic governance. To counter this, there is a need to champion the decentralization of governance, transferring more authority and decision-making power to local and regional entities. This shift would not only enhance the responsiveness of governance systems but also ensure that decisions are more attuned to the unique needs and contexts of diverse communities. Through such decentralization, we can foster a governance model that is truly representative, resilient, and resistant to overarching global dominance.

5. Fostering Open Dialogue: Building Bridges Beyond Borders

- **Cultivating Alternative International Forums:** In the shadow of the United Nations' expansive influence, there is an urgent need for alternative international platforms that champion authentic dialogue, free from the shackles of political motives and agendas. These forums must emphasize genuine conversation, collaboration, and mutual respect among nations. By doing so, they can counterbalance the often politically-charged atmosphere of the UN, ensuring a more diverse and inclusive global discourse that truly represents a myriad of perspectives and concerns.

- **Advancing Cultural Exchange Initiatives:** To build a world resistant to the dominance of monolithic entities like the UN, the promotion of cultural exchanges is vital. These exchanges transcend mere diplomatic formalities; they are about immersing in and understanding diverse cultural heritages. By experiencing and appreciating the rich tapestry of global cultures firsthand, individuals and communities can break down barriers of misunderstanding and prejudice. Such grassroots-level interactions lay the foundation for a world where political and cultural nuances are respected and celebrated, creating a global community that is interconnected yet not homogenized.

The path ahead, uncharted and rife with uncertainties, casts a spotlight on entities like the United Nations and their potential to significantly mold our world's future. Yet, it is crucial to recognize that the true power to shape this future doesn't rest solely in the hands of such global organizations. The collective will and voice of people worldwide hold the ultimate sway in dictating the course we take. By actively embracing measures that prioritize informed engagement, grassroots empowerment, transparency, and decentralized governance, we can steer towards a future that harmoniously blends unity with the rich tapestry of global diversity. This envisioned future is one where global cooperation doesn't equate to the loss of individual and cultural identities, and where the global narrative is shaped not by a singular entity, but by the diverse and collective aspirations of the world's populace.

<u>Epilogue</u>

As we venture into an era marked by unprecedented challenges and evolving global dynamics, it becomes increasingly clear that the path ahead is a complex intertwining of obstacles and potential breakthroughs. In navigating this terrain, it is imperative for nations and individuals alike to remain actively informed, critically engaged, and unwaveringly proactive. The delicate balance between fostering global cooperation and preserving the rich, distinctive fabric of individual societies is akin to a nuanced dance - a dance where the steps of unity and diversity must be in sync to orchestrate the symphony of the future.

In closing, it must be acknowledged that the United Nations, despite its initial promise of global unity and peace, has clearly veered from its founding vision. This deviation brings to the forefront the crucial responsibility that lies with nations and their citizens: to ensure that our shared future is not monopolized by a singular entity or agenda. Vigilance, critical awareness, and active participation are indispensable tools in steering the global community away from the precipice of a dystopian world. Instead, we should aim towards an era characterized by genuine collaboration, respect for sovereign identities, and collective prosperity. This is not merely an aspiration but an imperative - a commitment to guiding the world toward a future that truly embodies the spirit of cooperation, equitable growth, and mutual respect.

"As we close this chapter of insights and reflections, those seeking a comprehensive guide to a brighter, more equitable future will find a treasure trove of solutions in **'Reconstructing Reality: The Roadmap to Global Harmony: A Comprehensive Blueprint for a Just and Harmonious World.'** This seminal work provides a meticulously crafted plan for creating a world where justice, harmony, and the well-being of all are not just ideals, but achievable realities. It is a manifesto for those who believe in a better world for all."